FRANCIS FRITH'S

CARMARTHEN - A HISTORY AND CELEBRATION

THE FRANCIS FRITH COLLECTION

www.francisfrith.com

CARMARTHEN

A HISTORY AND CELEBRATION OF THE TOWN

WENDY HUGHES

Produced by The Francis Frith Collection

www.francisfrith.com

First published in the United Kingdom in 2004 by
The Francis Frith Collection®

Hardback Edition 2004 ISBN 1-90493-815-9
Paperback Edition 2011 ISBN 978-1-84589-620-1

British Library Cataloguing in Publication Data

Carmarthen - A History and Celebration of The Town
Wendy Hughes

The Francis Frith Collection®
Oakley Business Park, Wylye Road,
Dinton, Wiltshire SP3 5EU
Tel: +44 (0) 1722 716 376
Email: info@francisfrith.co.uk
www.francisfrith.com

Printed and bound in Great Britain
Contains material sourced from responsibly managed forests

Front Cover: **CARMARTHEN, CORACLES 1898** 41093t

Additional photographs by Conrad Hughes.
Domesday extract used in timeline by kind permission of Alecto Historical Editions, www.domesdaybook.org.

Aerial photographs reproduced under licence from Simmons Aerofilms Limited.
Historical Ordnance Survey maps reproduced under licence from Homecheck.co.uk

The colour-tinting in this book is for illustrative purposes only, and is not intended to be historically accurate

AS WITH ANY HISTORICAL DATABASE, THE FRANCIS FRITH ARCHIVE IS CONSTANTLY BEING CORRECTED AND IMPROVED, AND THE PUBLISHERS WOULD WELCOME INFORMATION ON OMISSIONS OR INACCURACIES

Contents

CARMARTHEN FROM THE AIR 1961 AFA96229

Historical Timeline for Carmarthen

Roman Britain

49BC Julius Caesar crosses the Rubicon

AD74 Romans build fort at Moridunum

AD79 Eruption of Vesuvius destroying Pompeii

AD117-138 Moridunum becomes a civitas capital

AD122 Emperor Hadrian orders Hadrian's Wall to be built

AD455 Vandals sack Rome

Dark Ages

AD520 Possible period of King Arthur legend

Some time during the Dark Ages the Celtic monastic church of Llandeulyddog is built

AD871 King Alfred and Danelaw

Tudor Britain

1485 Sir Rhys ap Thomas knighted at Bosworth Field by Henry VII

1509 Henry VIII becomes king

1537 Dissolution of the Priory of St John

1538 Dissolution of the Grey Friars

1543 First Grammar School founded

1546 Royal charter making Carmarthen a corporate Borough

1555 Dr Robert Farrar, Bishop of St David's, burnt at the stake in Market Square

1558 Accession of Elizabeth 1

1576 Queen Elizabeth Grammar School founded

1588 Span- ish Armada defeated

1600 Founding of East India Company

Stuart Britain

1603 New charter raising Carmarthen's status to County Borough

1605 Gunpowder Plot

1644 Carmarthen surrenders to Cromwell

1649 Cromwell visits Carmarthen

1649 Charles I executed

1666 Great Fire of London

Victorian Britain

1837 Victo- ria becomes queen

1843 Rebecca Riots: the workhouse is attacked

1846 Repeal of Corn Laws

1848 South Wales and Monmouthshire Training College (Trinity College) opens

1851 Nott's Monument erected

1851 Great Exhibition at Crystal Palace

1852 Railway arrives at Carmarthen

1854 Public or Assembly Rooms open

1865 Last pleasure steamer launched from the Quay

1881 First Boer War

1885 Karl Benz designs first automobile

1895 Girls' Grammar School founded

1900 Carmarthen Park and cycle track opened

1901 Queen Victoria dies

Edwardian Era

1903 Campaign for women's suffrage begins

1905 American trick cyclist at Carmarthen Park

1906 Boer War monument erected in Guildhall Square

1910 National Eisteddfod Proclamation Ceremony at Carmarthen Park

1910 Edward VII dies

Middle Ages

110-1135 Castle built

1107-1115 St Peter's church given to Battle Abbey

1125 St Peter's Church given to the Priory of St John and St Teulyddog

1180 Carmarthen receives its first royal charter

1233 First Norman town wall built

1270 Franciscan Friary (Greyfriars) founded

1066 Battle of Hastings. Norman rule begins

1086 Domesday Book

1170 Murder of Thomas à Becket at Canterbury cathedral

1215 Magna Carta

1306 Robert the Bruce declares himself King of Scotland

Late Medieval

1326 Carmarthen selected as a Staple town for the export of goods

1349 Black Death arrives in Carmarthen

1360 John Andrew Spilman becomes Carmarthen's first recorded mayor

1360-1403 Owain Glyndwr attacks the town and castle

1415 New Norman town wall built covering a larger area

1348 Black Death kills 25 million in Europe

1415 Battle of Agincourt

1485 Battle of Bosworth Field marks end of Plantaganet dynasty

Georgian Era

1718 Isaac Carter brings his printing press to Carmarthen

1763 John Wesley preaches on Castle Green

1770 Political battles in the streets of Carmarthen

1796 Wynveth Stream covered over

1818 Cheese riots at the Quay

1822 Gas lamps light the streets of Carmarthen

1739 John Wesley founds Methodist church

1762 Mozart performs at the age of 6

1789 French Revolution

1815 Battle of Waterloo

1825 Stockton to Darlington Railway

20th Century Britain

1911 Brinley Richards plaque unveiled in Hall Street

1918 Lyric opened as a concert and cinema hall

1936 Carmarthen's coat of arms granted to the borough by the College of Heralds

1938 Bridge into the town opened

1940 10,000 children evacuated to Carmarthen

1951 Last Quarter Sessions in Carmarthen

1957 Women enrolled at Trinity College

1966 Gwynfor Evans became first Plaid Cymru Member of Parliament

1974 National Eisteddfod held in Carmarthen

2000 The graves of George III's granddaughter and great-granddaughter discovered at St Peter's Church

1914 First World War begins

1926 John Logie Baird obtains first television picture

1939 Outbreak of Second World War

1956 Suez Crisis

1966 England win World Cup

1969 First man on the Moon

1982 Falklands Conflict

CHAPTER ONE

The Birth of a Town

CARMARTHENSHIRE is a lush green county, mainly agricultural, comprised of rolling hills set in a countryside flecked with sheep and cattle, wild flowers and prehistoric monuments. Ancient trees cast watchful eyes over its inhabitants, whilst a wealth of mystery and history weave a colourful tapestry. At the heart of the county sits the ancient town of Carmarthen, known to the Romans as Moridunum, and located on the banks of the river Towy (28123), once Carmarthen's primary route to the outside world. In fact, the port was so important that by 1353 it was authorised to sell to foreign parts the five staple commodities: wool, pelts (skins with the fleece on), leather, lead and tin. Ships imported and exported goods through the tidal Towy estuary from the Bristol Channel, as well as taking emigrants to new and exciting lands, helping Carmarthen to become and remain a vibrant town.

It is said that people make a town, and this is certainly true of Carmarthen, for here you will find a relaxed atmosphere where the Welsh and English languages sit comfortably together. Local people have a deep commitment to their history and culture, and yet they enjoy the facilities of a modern shopping centre.

THE RIVER TOWY 1890 28123

The river played in important role in the history of Carmarthen. Note its distinctive horseshoe bend. In the distance are the rolling hills.

CORACLES 1898 41093t

This photograph was obviously taken during the fishing season between mid-April and mid-June, and at a time when there were no restrictions on the numbers who could fish. In the 1860s there were about 400 coracle men operating on the Towy.

Very little is known of the early history of Carmarthen, but the embryonic town probably evolved from a Celtic hill-fort built on what is known as Merlin's Hill. By the time the Romans reached west Wales, a Celtic Goidelic tribe originating from Ireland had established a fortress camp overlooking the river on Castle Hill. But even before the Romans, the river was home to the coracle, a small fishing boat (41093). Today only twelve pairs are licensed to fish for sea trout (sewin) on the Towy; they operate mostly at night between Carmarthen Town and the mouth of the river, three miles upstream from Ferryside.

In AD74 the Romans built their most westerly fort where a busy road came to a port. The name Moridunum, meaning sea fort, is derived from the old Celtic Brythonic 'mori' (sea) and 'dunon' (fort). This civil settlement became an important self-governing city, one of only two in Wales, with its distinctive 'playing card' layout on the eastern side of the fort; it was later enclosed within a defensive rampart with ditches. The

Coracle Fishing

Coracle fishing is a tradition that is handed down from one generation to another. The boat is light and made from canvas or calico stretched over a framework of ash lathes, which requires good basket-making skills. It is made waterproof by using pitch and tar. When Carmarthen was the centre of the woollen trade, Welsh flannel was stretched over the framework and covered with three coats of tar, but when flannel became expensive, calico was used. The coracle is carried on the fisherman's back with a strap fixed to the seat. Once in the boat, the fishermen work in pairs with a net suspended between them. Each man holds one end of the net and controls the coracle with a single oar. In this picture we see William Elias and his son, also William; they were a well-known coracle-fishing family.

CORACLE FISHING ON THE TOWY c1950 C31031x

military fort was discovered in 1989 spanning Spilman Street and King Street; it had a pebbled street around the inside perimeter, allowing access to a fighting platform along the rampart bank, together with timber barracks buildings. At some later date a smaller fort was built within the larger one, indicating that the garrison had been reduced. Earlier excavations throughout this part of the town uncovered a tanning pit, several buildings, pottery, and a worn coin of the Emperor Domitian (AD 81-96), as well as a trumpet brooch in silver gilt of the Romano-Celtic period dated AD25-50. When St Peter's churchyard was removed for road-widening, both Flavian and Samian ware were discovered, together with some decorated bowls, cooking jars, and vessels used for the storage of wine and oils. All these items, along with several bracelets and glass beads, can be seen

THE CORACLE FISHERMAN c1950 C31033

William Elias senior received the British Empire Medal for services to coracle fishing.

in Carmarthen Museum. One of the most curious discoveries was of a dodecahedron, a twelve-sided bronze object, discovered in 1768. Its use remains a mystery, although several theories have been put forward, including that it was a gauge used in a workshop, or even a twelve-sided candlestick. It has recently been suggested that it was used as a surveying instrument. A large town house, complete with under-floor heating, was discovered during the building of St Peter's car park.

Did you know?

The only Roman inscribed stone yet to be found is the so-called 'Nato' stone, bearing the inscription '(bon)o r(ei)p(uplica) nato', thought to allude to a 4th-century emperor. Two Roman altars or pedestals have been found, and one of these is now in the porch of St Peter's Church, the other, together with the 'Nato 'stone, is in Carmarthen Museum.

ROMAN ALTAR OR PEDESTAL IN THE PORCH OF ST PETER'S 2004 C31701k (Conrad Hughes)

A settlement grew up outside the east gate of the military fort. Here, for around 200 years, craftsmen traded their wares in this busy artisan quarter, and trades like blacksmithing, iron production, the manufacture of leather goods, and bread and beer making were carried out. Suddenly the people of Carmarthen would have undergone a culture shock as they watched their small farming community, previously growing barley and wheat, and existing on a diet of milk, cheese, butter and meat, become transformed into a world of luxurious town life, with an influx of new consumer goods, such as wine, olive oil, fine pottery, exotic jewellery and paved floors. Shops and markets developed, and bartering was replaced with Roman coins for trading.

Whilst Caerwent (Venta Silurum) in the east became the tribal capital of the Silures in Glamorgan, Moridunum, the only defended town in the tribal area of the Demetae, became the civitas capital of the Demetae tribe in the west. This was a feature common in Roman Britain: the Romans were keen to maintain the tribal systems they found, and to adapt them to their civil administration, encouraging local leaders to become Romanised citizens. We are not sure when Moridunum became the tribal capital, but it may have been during the reign of Emperor Hadrian (AD117-138), who visited Britain around AD121 to withdraw troops from Wales to help construct his famous frontier wall in the north. Excavations show that Moridunum military fort was reduced, and then abandoned by AD120, suggesting it was made a civitas capital in Hadrian's time. Moridunum was important enough to have its own amphitheatre (C31702k), one of only seven in Britain, with timber seating in step formation for up to five thousand people. This capacity was well in excess of the town's population, so it would seem that the amphitheatre served the people living in the surrounding tribal areas, and would have been the focal point for many a spectacular event. Today the boundary defences of Moridunum can still be seen along the Esplanade, The Parade, Parade Road, Little Water Street, Richmond Terrace and Old Oak Lane. Priory Street, the oldest street in Carmarthen, was the main road running straight through Roman Moridunum.

THE ROMAN AMPHITHEATRE 2004 C31702k (Conrad Hughes)

Carmarthen is proud of its heritage, as we can see from this well-kept site.

SIGN OUTSIDE THE AMPHITHEATRE 2004
C31703k (Conrad Hughes)

There is no evidence to indicate continuous settlement in Carmarthen into the so-called Dark Ages. We do know that the succeeding centuries saw the advent of the early Christian church, and several references in the book of Liber Landavensis suggest that Llandeulyddog, a Celtic monastic Church, was founded in the town. It is possible that there were Roman buildings on the site of St Peter's Church, which is the oldest building in Carmarthen still used for its original purpose. There is no written evidence of St Peter's Church until around 1100; then, between 1107 and 1115, it was given to Battle Abbey. In 1125 St Peter's was given to the Priory of St John and St Teulyddog, a monastery located at the other end of Priory Street.

Little remains of the priory today except the gatehouse, which is built into a house at the bottom end of Old Priory Road. The site is interesting because it sits to the south-east of Roman Moridunum, just outside the Roman walls, and to the south of Priory Street, which most probably follows the Roman road as it

ST PETER'S CHURCH 1910 62622

St Peter's is built of local limestone, old red sandstone and grey shale stone, and the building can seat up to 870 people. The organ was originally ordered by King George III for Windsor Castle, but it was brought to St Peter's in 1796.

ST PETER'S CHURCH, THE INTERIOR 1925 77297

entered the town's east gate. This area could have been the site of a Roman cemetery, as these were often located along the roads just outside the towns, and could have continued as a Christian burial ground in the early Christian period, so this could be where the Celtic monastic settlement of Llandeulyddog was located.

The present-day name of Carmarthen is derived from Moridunum with the Welsh prefix 'Caer' added – 'caer' means a Roman fort. Through the passage of time Caer-Myrddin became associated with Myrddin or Merlin, the famous wizard, prophet, magician, and guardian of King Arthur. According to legend, Myrddin was born in Carmarthen, and lived in a cave deep in Bryn Myrddin, Merlin's Hill (see page 19).

It is claimed that after wandering in misery for some fifty years Merlin became a prophet, and from the 9th century onwards his prophecies were remembered in poems said to have been written by him. Legend informs us that Merlin was imprisoned in Bryn Myrddin by Vivien, to whom he had taught his magic spells. Unfortunately the exact location of the cave is lost, but it is said that Merlin can be heard lamenting his folly in letting a woman learn his secret spells, and groaning as he tries to release himself from the chains that hold him deep within the cave. Today, the Merlin Hill Centre is situated at Alltyfyrddin. Here visitors can follow in the footsteps of Merlin the wizard and walk up the ancient paths to the site of the Iron Age hill-fort, and listen for Merlin's ghostly wailings!

Anne Vaughan

St Peter's Church contains the largest collection of memorials in the county – some can be seen in photograph 77297. The oldest monument inside the building is to Anne, the second wife of Sir William Vaughan of Golden Grove and Torycoed, Llangendeirne. She married Sir William in 1616, and had six children. She is shown kneeling in prayer, for it is said that this is how she was found when she died at the age of 84, kneeling at her bedside.

MEMORIAL AND EFFIGY OF ANNE VAUGHAN
2004 C31704k (Conrad Hughes)

The Old Oak

There are numerous legends about Merlin which centre around Carmarthen. Merlin prophesied that 'When Priory Oak shall tumble down, then shall fall Carmarthen town.' Efforts were made to preserve the tree when it began to wither - but some say it was deliberately poisoned by a resident who became annoyed at youngsters congregating around it. Concrete was poured into the withering stump, and steel bands held it together, until eventually in 1978 it was taken down - and Carmarthen Town held her breath! What is left of the Old Oak used to be displayed in a glass case in the foyer of St Peter's Civic Centre, but at the time of writing, it is resting safely within the council offices awaiting a new glass case. No doubt it will be on display very soon.

THE OLD OAK 1949 C31052p

THE OLD OAK 2004 C31706k (Conrad Hughes)

MERLIN'S HILL 2004 C317105k (Conrad Hughes)

Did you know?

Tales about Merlin were exploited by the local people, including an old widow, who in the early 19th century used to show tourists around a house in Priory Street, which was reputed to have been the home of Merlin.

THE TOWY VALLEY FROM THE PARADE 1893 32785

The third hill from the right is Merlin's Hill.

Almost seven hundred years after the Romans left Britain, the Normans came to Carmarthen, where they found a Welsh religious community. They fortified the town with a motte and bailey castle on a hill above the River Towy, where County Hall now stands. The first reference to it states that Castle 'Rhyd-y-gors' was built in 1093 under the command of William Rufus. It was replaced by a stone castle in the reign of Henry I (1100-1135). Under the shadow of the castle grew the Norman town, which flourished alongside it; but it was very distinct from the existing community.

The old settlement, or Old Town, consisted of the native Welsh community which had grown up around the monastic settlement centred on the old Celtic church; this was now administered by the powerful Augustinian priory of St John the Evangelist, founded by the Black Canons. In contrast, the New Town, which was eventually surrounded by town walls, was under the authority of the royal castle. A market was established outside the castle's main gate, and from this small settlement of traders and artisans the town evolved around the market place.

THE CASTLE GATEWAY 2004 C31707k (Conrad Hughes)

This is all that remains today of the castle gateway. Restoration work is being carried out at the moment.

As you can imagine, there was endless conflict between the two settlements. Separate charters were granted to each town; the first was granted by King John in 1201. The castle was captured many times: it was destroyed by the Welsh Prince Owain Gwynedd, and rebuilt by the Earl of Pembroke, only to be lost again to the Welsh after a siege, and recaptured by Henry II, who then lost it to Llewellyn ap Iorwerth. It was later recaptured after a three-month siege, which heralded the building of the town wall in 1233. The first area enclosed by the wall was quite small - it roughly included the present day Nott Square, Guildhall Square, Bridge Street, Quay Street and the castle site. There were four gates: Bridge Gate, Towy Gate, Wynveth Gate, later to be called Dark Gate, and the East Gate - later called the Prisoners' Gate. It is thought that much of the stone used for the gates was robbed from the ruins of Roman Moridunum.

During the 13th century the castle was remodelled using the most up-to-date military architecture; a stone bridge replaced the timber bridge into the town, which had been built by the Romans. Henry III ordered new shops to be built 'in the midst of our town of Kermerdyn' to the west of the church of St Mary. From this we know that a church was in existence before 1252, and stood on the north side of the market place, near the medieval market cross. All that remains today of St Mary's is a window set into the left wall of the Angel Vaults in Nott Square, opposite the castle gate (C31708k).

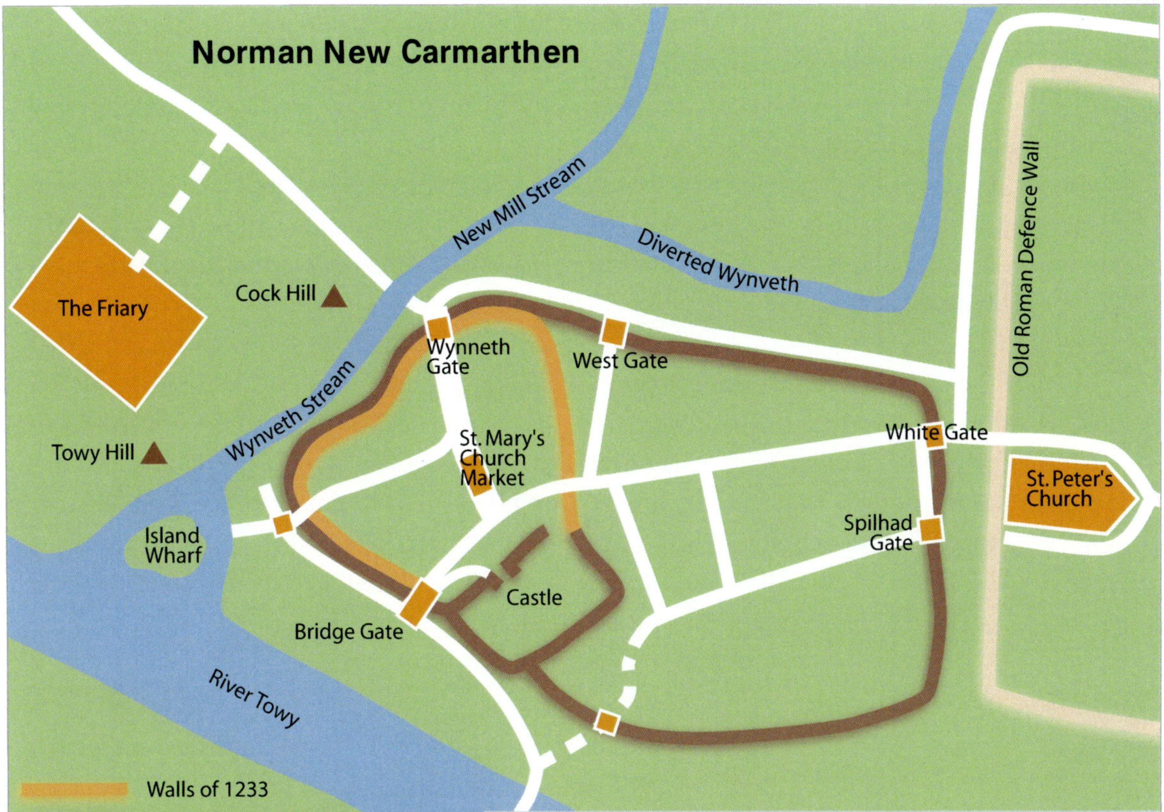

MAP OF NORMAN CARMARTHEN 2004 ZZZ00759 (Wendy Hughes)

ST MARY'S WINDOW 2004 C31708k (Conrad Hughes)

We also know that there were several water mills located outside the walls, and we learn from an early survey that one 'Daniel the Miller of Kermerdyn' owned and erected his own mill, paying five shillings a year to the bailiffs. It is thought that this mill stood between the Wynveth Gate and the river Towy, and became known later as Towy Mill.

Little is known about the common lands of New Carmarthen, but it is believed that strips of land used for cultivation lay on either side of a trackway known today as Lammas Street, which emerged at Wynveth Gate onto land belonging to the royal castle.

Lammas Fields, as it was called, became the site of a Franciscan friary a few years later. These fields were thrown open as common pasture land on Lammas Day (loaf-mass day, 1 August) until planting the following spring, hence the name. Lammas was also the day when the church held a harvest festival, where loaves of bread made from the ripe corn were consecrated.

Two of the earliest recorded burgess families are still remembered in the names of two of the town's main streets, King Street and Spilman Street. A William Kyng is mentioned in 1197 along with Robert Spilman, who witnessed a document giving Abernant church to the priory. Other Spilmans are recorded in documents belonging to the priory; for instance, an entry dated 1270 names Andrew Spilman as witness to an exchange of land, whilst in the 1360s a later member of the family, John Andrew Spilman, is referred to as mayor, one of the earliest recorded holders of the office in Carmarthen. King Street originated as a trackway between the Norman New Town and the Old Carmarthen Town. This area was not enclosed within the first town walls of 1233, but became so within a later wall of 1415, with a new gateway, White Gate, positioned at the St Peter's end of the street. The first documented evidence of Spilman Street (C31059) occurs in 1355, when 'Spylmanstret' is mentioned.

SPILMAN STREET 1949 C31059

Hostility continued between the two towns. This led to the burgesses of New Town lodging a complaint to Edward II around 1315. They were concerned that the priory and its tenants were buying and selling goods in Old Town and not paying tolls on the movement of goods, conducting unfair trading on such goods as wool and skins, using weights and measures of their own, and running a market and fair without a King's warrant. The Prior was ordered to produce a royal warrant, and when he failed to do so, the burgesses of the New Town petitioned the King. Once again the Prior was ordered to produce a warrant, but he protested, claiming that his people had been allowed to buy and sell for as long as he could remember. Finally, in 1318 Edward II acknowledged the Prior's rights to hold a market in Old Town; but again in 1330 the burgesses of New Town complained. The animosity continued for years. In 1353, their reeve, Thomas Japhes, went into the Old Town to collect tolls, and was promptly thrown into prison by the Prior!

The river has always played its part in the growth of the town, particularly in the Middle Ages, when it was the main transport route. Ships sailed up the Towy, initially bringing goods such as wine from Gascony and Portugal to the castle, and sailed back taking wool, hides, pelts, leather, and tin for export. In 1326 Carmarthen was selected as a staple town for the export of these goods; there had been a long-standing custom of levying a tax on them, to make it easier for the King's officials to collect the revenue. The quality of the goods was checked, and fair trading was guaranteed under royal supervision. By the Ordinance of the Staple, 1353, Carmarthen became the only staple town in Wales, giving it a huge advantage over other Welsh ports.

New Town continued to thrive and expand until an outbreak of the Black Death took its toll in the late 1340s. Being a trading port Carmarthen was susceptible, and the officials of the Staple were among the first of many victims within the town in 1349. Consequently many of the rents owed by the burgesses of the town to the Crown went unpaid, and it took Carmarthen many years to recover.

During the second half of the 14th century, the mention in the records of some of Carmarthen's older streets indicates that there was some development of the area between Old and New Town, along King Street and Spilman Street, which lay outside the walls of New Town. In 1355 Edward, the Black Prince, claimed that the area between 'Halogyn' (possibly modern day Little Water Street), which is 'a certain lane and pool unto the Walls of the New Town', was part of New Town annexed by Edward I and did not belong to the priory. In his response, the Prior successfully rejected the claim, with specific references to Spylmanstret and Sutternstreet (possibly King Street). The pool mentioned could have been the Wynveth stream, which had been diverted in the previous century to run along what is now Little Water Street to present day Woods Row to protect the growing north side of the New Town.

All this unrest led to many quarrels of Welsh versus Welsh and Welsh verses Normans, resulting in the castle being captured and recaptured and the town being razed to the ground on many occasions. The men of Carmarthen were present at many of the great battles, such as Bannockburn (1314), Crecy (1346) and the siege of Calais (1347), with Carmarthen ships being commandeered for the King's service to transport troops or to chase the enemy from the Welsh coast.

The beginning of the 15th century saw many towns affected by Owain Glyn Dwr's revolt. When Carmarthenshire rebelled in 1403, the Sheriff of Somerset was ordered 'to leave all else and without excuse to load ships with wine, ale, floure, salt, fish and convey them to Carmarthen' for supplying to the army. On 5 July 1403 Owain Glyn Dwr attacked the town and castle again, ransacking the priory and destroying its archives and title deeds. Houses were burnt down in Spilman Street, and in the New Town burgesses were robbed and their properties destroyed in the attack. In all, fifty townspeople were killed. The castle surrendered to Owain Glyn Dwr, but he subsequently withdrew from the town, and in September of that year Henry VI visited and stayed in Carmarthen for five days, when he ordered the castle defences to be strengthened. However, by 1405 Owain Glyn Dwr was back. He recaptured the town and castle, but in the following year royal power was restored; the rebellion died out, but the effects lingered for many years with a decline in the fortunes of the port.

Large sums of money were spent to repair the castle, and in 1415, in the reign of Henry V, a grant of £20 a year was made to the town for a new wall to be built. The wall was begun in 1415 and enclosed a much larger area, which included Spilman Street and King Street, although Lammas Street still remained outside the walls. The new wall ran along the same course as the old wall to the Wynveth Gate (Dark Gate), and as there is no further evidence of a wall it has been surmised that it must have run to a gateway, traditionally known as West Gate, which has now disappeared. From there it ran parallel to Woods Row, then behind Little Water Street to a new gateway, called White Gate, at the end of King Street; then it went along Conduit Lane to the Spilman Gate, which was destroyed in 1768, and continued along the back of the properties in Parade Road, and then south-west to Dan-y-Banc. Two stretches of this wall can be seen at the rear of the Ivy Bush Hotel and behind the District Council Offices. From Dan-y-Banc the wall would have joined up with the castle, but as this was cleared when Castle Hill was constructed in 1804, nothing of the original remains.

The greatly enlarged New Town now lay side by side with the Old Town, and this medieval lay-out of streets with narrow lanes and winding alley-ways remained almost unchanged within the town's boundaries until present day, although there was some expansion outside Carmarthen's medieval walls. By the end of this period a birds-eye view of Carmarthen would have shown the towers and walls of the castle,

TILE MURAL IN GREYFRIARS SHOPPING CENTRE 2004 ZZZ00761 (Conrad Hughes)

A birds-eye view of Carmarthen showing the substantial friary.

the various gateways cut into the town walls, with the ruins of Roman ramparts of Old Town with its priory to the east. St Peter's Church was on the western tip, whilst St Mary's Church stood in the centre of New Town, and the Friary outside the town walls on its western skirt.

Much of the early history of Carmarthen is associated with the religious houses of the town, the Priory of St John and the Franciscan Friary. These were also the earliest seats of learning in the town, and over the years they were followed by a number of schools, including the Queen Elizabeth Grammar School for Boys, which was founded in 1576.

The old Priory, an Augustinian foundation of Black Canons, stood near the river, just off Priory Street, and was the virtual ruler of the Old Town. It enjoyed many privileges, such as its own markets and fairs (it obtained its first charter in 1180) and a system of courts, and it gained its revenue from several churches, including St Peter's Church. The Black Book of Carmarthen (Llyfr Du Caerfyddin), the oldest surviving manuscript of Welsh language poetry and one of Wales's most precious treasures, was written at the Priory. The Black Book is so named because of the colour of its binding and its connection with the Black Canons of the Priory of St John the Evangelist and St Teulyddog. It is thought to be the work of one Welsh scribe writing at different periods in his life up to 1250 - the oldest part of the book was written in the 12th century. It is a collection of poems, mythology and history belonging to a still older period. Today it is kept in the National Library of Wales in Aberystwyth.

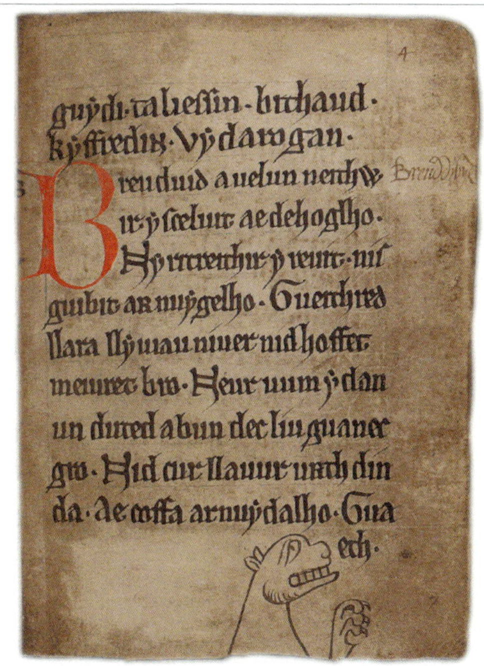

THE BLACK BOOK OF CARMARTHEN ZZZ00760

Cyhoeddwyd gan Lyfrgell Genedlaethol Cymru gyda nawdd cyngor Tref Caerfyrddin ©2000

published by the National Library of Wales with the support of Carmarthen Town Council ©2000

The Friary

Around 1270 the Franciscan Friary (Greyfriars) was founded to the west of the New Town. It was one of the largest Franciscan Friaries in Britain, certainly the largest in Wales. Many of the friars were master herbalists; they created effective medicines from herbs and plants, which were used to cure the sick nursed by the friars working in the infirmary. The friars were also accomplished gardeners, cooks and bakers; they brewed alcoholic beverages and cider, and shared their produce amongst the less fortunate in Carmarthen.

However, with the dissolution of the Priory of St John by Henry VIII in 1537, Old Town was amalgamated with the New Town, forming a Corporate Borough. Subsequent charters were granted by James I in 1604 and by George III in 1764. The Priory was still visible in the 19th century, but it was demolished when a tin works was established, which in turn was demolished to make way for the railways.

DETAIL OF CARMARTHEN ORDNANCE SURVEY MAP 1886

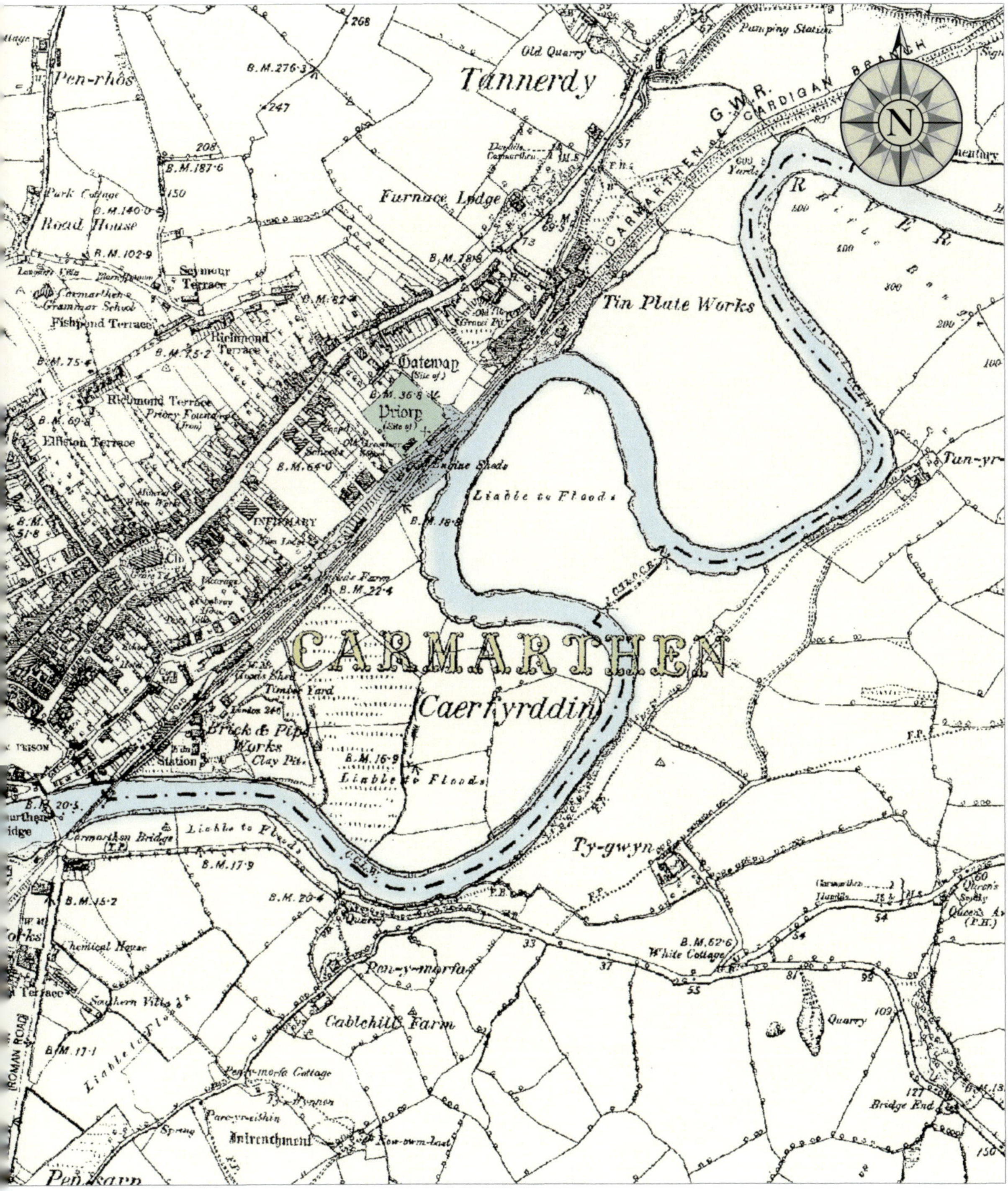

Map showing the Priory grounds and the railway and engine sheds intersecting them

CHAPTER TWO

Tudor Kings, Civil Wars and Riotous Mobs

WHEN HENRY Tudor succeeded to the throne as Henry VII in 1485, he brought with him a period of much-needed peace. Having been born in neighbouring Pembrokeshire, he proudly acknowledged his Welsh roots; he had been nursed by a Welsh foster-mother, and spoke the native language. He had many Welshmen in his court, and records show that in 1492 he gave his courtiers £2 to celebrate St David's Day. He also rewarded his Welsh supporters with royal positions and estates. One such person was Rhys ap Thomas, who among other offices became Mayor of Carmarthen on three occasions. He was instrumental in Henry's accession, because after Richard III was killed at Bosworth Field, Rhys ap Thomas placed the muddy crown of England upon the new king's head. In turn Henry knighted Sir Rhys on the battlefield with the sword that still bore the blood of the late King Richard, and from that day forward, Henry always called him 'Father Rhys'. Sir Rhys died in 1525 and was buried at the Friary in Carmarthen, but the tomb of Sir Rhys and his second wife, Janet, was later removed to St Peter's Church. In 1865 it underwent a total reconstruction by a direct descendant, Lord Dynevor. In 1886, the tomb was placed under the arch between the chancel and the consistory court, and it was finally moved to its present position (C31709k), although records mistakenly now gave the name of his first wife, Eva.

Under Sir Rhys, Carmarthen enjoyed a long period of peace, but Henry's policy to reduce the power of local barons in favour of strong central government meant that Sir Rhys was one of the last of the landed gentry to have such power.

Sir Rhys ap Thomas

Sir Rhys received rich estates in south west Wales from King Henry VII. He was also appointed Chamberlain (Treasurer) at Carmarthen Castle, and amongst his titles he was Chamberlain of Carmarthen and Cardigan, Chamberlain and Steward of Haverfordwest, Constable and Steward of Brecon, and Steward of Builth. He became Mayor of Carmarthen three times, and in 1505 he was created a Knight of the Garter and a Privy Councillor by Henry VII. When Henry VII died in 1509, Sir Rhys continued to serve Henry VIII; he was present at the Battle of the Spurs in France in 1513, as well as the Field of the Cloth of Gold in 1520. He was now seventy-one years old, and the virtual ruler of south west Wales. A popular saying at that time was: 'the king owns the whole island except that part which belongs to Sir Rhys'. In his will Sir Rhys left £20 to the Friars of Carmarthen, £6 13s 4d to the Priory, a vestment to St Mary's Church, and a chalice to St Peter's Church.

THE TOMB OF SIR RHYS AP THOMAS AND HIS WIFE IN ST PETER'S 2004

C31709k (Conrad Hughes)

TILE MURAL, THE GREYFRIARS SHOPPING CENTRE, DEPICTING SIR RHYS AP THOMAS 2004
ZZZ00761 (Conrad Hughes)

During the reign of Henry's infamous son, Henry VIII (1509-1547), the unification of England and Wales under the Acts of Union of 1536 and 1543 meant that Carmarthen became part of the new county of Carmarthenshire (it remained so until it was incorporated into Dyfed in 1974). For the first time Carmarthenshire was represented in Parliament at Westminster by a knight and by one burgess from the shire town of Carmarthen, but it also saw the dissolution of the Priory of St John in 1537, and of the Grey Friars at Friars Park in 1538, followed by the chantry chapels and St Mary's Church. The Priory was sold, whilst Carmarthen's first grammar school was founded at the Friary in 1543, beginning Carmarthen's long association with education.

In 1576 Queen Elizabeth Grammar School was founded with one master and one usher, and Latin, Greek and Theology were taught. Sir Thomas Powell's Charity school began in 1729 in three houses in Lower Market Street, now Hall Street, and moved to a new building to the east of the Esplanade which was built by subscription and dedicated in April 1847. These two schools amalgamated in 1857, and a new school building was built, by George Morgan and Sons, in 1884 between Richmond Terrace and Wellfield Road.

Although the school is renowned for its academic activities, it is also well known for producing some excellent sporting personalities, such as Gerald Davies, Ray Gravell and Roy Bergiers, who all played through the 'Golden 1970s'. Roy Bergiers also made a name for himself as the try scorer for Llanelli when they defeated the All Blacks at Strady in 1972. Rugby was not the only sport, as the school also had a gymnasium, and boxing was taught. Also, note the tennis courts in the foreground of picture 77295 (page 32), another sport played at the school.

The Grammar School

THE GRAMMAR SCHOOL 1925 77295

PLAQUE OUTSIDE THE OLD QUEEN ELIZABETH GRAMMAR SCHOOL FOR BOYS 2004
ZZZ00763 (Conrad Hughes)

With the end of the Priory came the amalgamation of the Old and New Towns, which in turn paved the way for a new charter in 1546, making Carmarthen a corporate borough, effectively putting an end to the rivalry between the two towns. Under this new charter the mayor was also appointed Admiral of the Port, confirming the importance of Carmarthen as a port, although by now the silting up of the river was causing some difficulty.

Did you know?

Carmarthen is the only town in Wales to have the privilege (by Royal Grant in 1546) of carrying a sword before its mayor on state occasions. The sword is carried unsheathed during war time and in its scabbard in times of peace. Also included in the corporation regalia is a replica silver oar, the symbol of the office of Admiral of the Port, granted to the mayor by Henry VIII, and still held by the Mayor of Carmarthen. Each May there is a river procession from Carmarthen to Ferryside to enable the mayor to assert his or her rights as Admiral of the Port.

In Tudor times the quay, with the Wynveth stream running on either side of the wharf, was located at Island Wharf, a strip of land which became an island at high tide (the present-day quay was not constructed until 1808). The market place was still outside the gateway to the castle, and it was here that Bishop Robert Farrar was burnt at the stake on the south side of the market cross.

Before the dissolution of the monasteries, Robert Farrar had been an Augustinian monk and a Prior in his native Yorkshire; then he joined the reformers, and through Archbishop Cranmer was appointed Bishop of St David's in 1548. Farrar quarrelled with his canons, accusing them of selling church property and bribery, and in return the canons accused him of being over-zealous in Protestant reforms. One of the charges brought against him was that when George Constantine, the reforming Archdeacon of Carmarthen and vicar of St Peter's Church, took down the high altar and replaced it with a communion table, Dr Farrar ordered Constantine to put it back in the chancel. Farrar was arrested, and was still in prison when the Roman Catholic Mary Tudor came to the throne in 1553. In 1554 he was dispossessed of his bishopric and tried in London. He refused to confess, and was brought back to Carmarthen for further trial before Bishop Henry Morgan, his successor at St David's, and George Constantine. It is ironic that Dr Farrar was imprisoned in Edward's VI's reign for not being enough of a Protestant reformer, and executed in Queen Mary's reign for refusing to renounce his Protestant faith.

THE CONSISTORY COURT AT ST PETER'S CHURCH 2004
C31710k (Conrad Hughes)

St Peter's is the only church in Wales to have a Consistory Court, and it is not known why there is one here. The Court and the bishop's chair on a raised dais and the pews all date from 1885. The court is presided over by the bishop to deal with cases of church law.

In 1842 a monument was erected in St Peter's Church in memory of Bishop Farrar (C31711k), and in 1902 a memorial tablet was placed within the railings of Nott's memorial bearing the inscription:

The noble army of Martyrs praise thee
Near the spot suffered for the truth
Saturday 30th March 1555
Dr Robert Farrar Bishop of St David's.
We shall by God's grace light such a candle in England, as shall never be put out.
Erected by a Protestant of this Town.

THE BISHOP FARRAR MEMORIAL IN ST PETER'S CHURCH 2004 C31711k (Conrad Hughes)

Did you know?

The stone that supported the stake on which Dr Robert Farrar, Bishop of St David's, was burnt now forms part of the summit of the church spire at Abergwili.

A glimpse into the surviving records from this period reveals much about the town. For example, we learn that in the reign of Elizabeth I, Carmarthen was the largest town in the area with 328 households and a population of over 2,000, whereas Llanelli was a mere hamlet of 12 households! In 1576, following complaints about weights, all wool bought and sold within the town was brought to the Guild Hall to be weighed. In 1580 we learn that Robert Toye paid rent for a shop under the Guildhall, and by 1582 a 'shambles' (meat market) also was held under the Guildhall. We learn that there were many trade guilds in the town, such as tanners, glovers, weavers, saddlers, cloth finishers, goldsmiths, silversmiths, cutlers and tinkers to name but a few, proving that Carmarthen was the hub of a thriving commercial community carrying on traditions starting in Roman times and continuing through to Norman times.

THE RIVERSIDE 1893 32772

The Elizabethan Port books for Carmarthen are interesting too, for they tell the story of a time when 28 ships and at least 63 merchants operated in the town. The merchants lived in the fashionable areas of the town, such as St Mary's Street, Quay Street and King Street, and whilst none of their houses survive, their names live on as the early governors in the Charter of the Queen Elizabeth Grammar School, founded in July 1576.

During the middle ages the quay was at Island Wharf, to the left of this picture, where the Wynveth flowed into the Towy. Buildings along the quay were regularly flooded at spring tides and times of heavy rain.

However, another side of Carmarthen includes the pirates and smugglers operating in the Bristol Channel; it would seem that some of Carmarthen's merchants were happy to conduct business with them. In 1587 a French ship laden with salt was seized by pirates and brought into Carmarthen, where the spoils were bought by Robert Toye and Edward Middleton, both former mayors of the town! We also discover that in 1592, the town's merchants complained to the Court of the Admiralty that they were robbed by pirates of silks, velvets, wine and oil to the value of £10,000, a substantial amount in those days.

With the death of Queen Elizabeth in 1603 the Tudor period ended, but with the Stuart James I came a new charter for Carmarthen, raising its status to County Borough. This meant that the town became a county in its own right with the formal title of the County Borough of Carmarthen; its burgesses could now choose its mayor and twenty council members, as well as its own Member of Parliament. This original charter, written in Latin and complete with the Great Seal, hangs in the Mayor's Parlour today.

John Speed's Carmarthen

A look at the earliest known map of Carmarthen, by John Speed and dated 1610, reveals that within the walls little had changed from the medieval period. Bridge Street and Towy Gates have been removed, probably to help the flow of trade to and from the busy quay area. Within the walls the map shows King Street and Spilman Street, with the castle's main gateway facing the market cross, with the stocks close by. The present Guildhall Square is named St Maries (St Mary's) Street, and two preaching crosses are shown, one in Lammas Street and the other in Priory Street - both crosses have now disappeared.

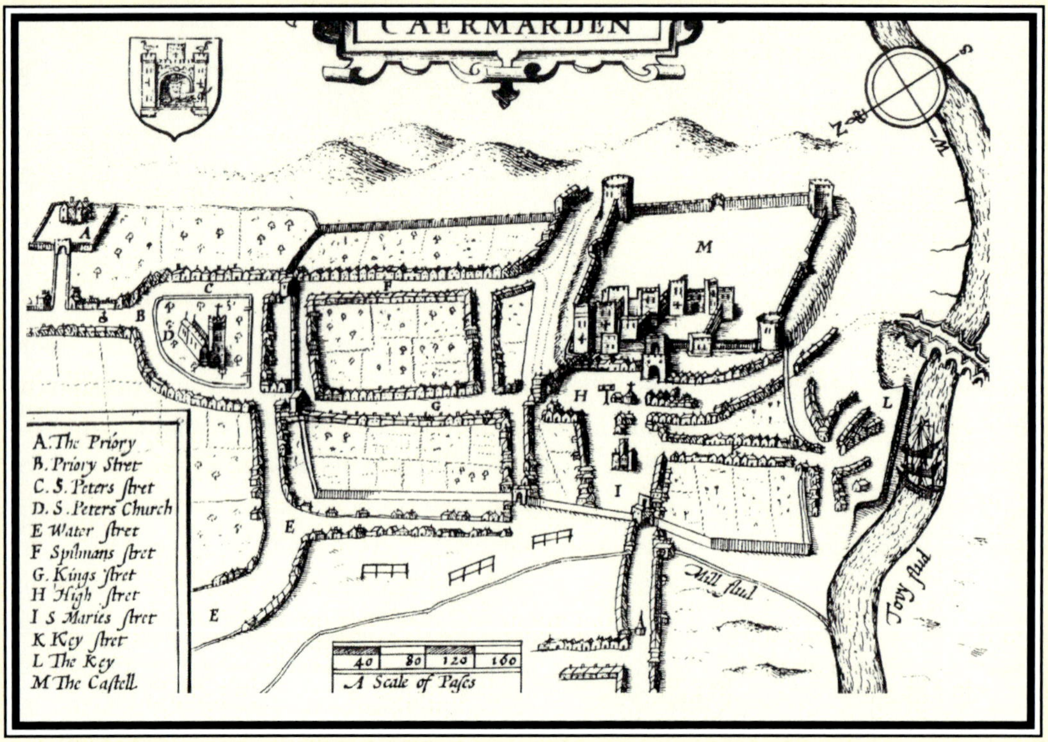

JOHN SPEED'S MAP OF 1610 ZZZ00764 (Reproduced by kind permission of Carmarthen Library)

THE BULWARKS 2004 C31712k (Conrad Hughes)

The Bulwarks can be seen from Morfa Lane. To the right are the Police Headquarters at Friar Park.

With so many narrow streets, we can assume fire must have been a problem for the town, because in 1633, the Corporation Order Books mention that Mayor Thomas Atkyns presented the town with twelve buckets with hooks and iron heads (used for pulling thatch off the roof) and iron chains.

Like most of Wales, Carmarthen was not really interested in the struggles of the new king, Charles I, although at one time Carmarthen was royalist, stemming from its loyalty to the Tudors. The leader of the Royalists in Carmarthenshire was Richard Vaughan of Golden Grove. However, after some successes in 1643 by the Parliamentary forces in neighbouring Pembrokeshire under General Rowland Laugharne, the Royalists were forced to withdraw, and Carmarthen surrendered in April 1644. A record dated from this time refers to 'the towne of Carmarthen fortified with a mudd wall round it.' This refers to the Bulwarks (C31712k), the Civil War defences consisting of a ditch and bank, reputed to be the finest examples of their kind in the country and still well kept today; they were hurriedly put up to defend the west and north side of the town, the area lying outside the medieval town walls.

The second phase of the war found General Laugharne changing sides to support the King in 1648, together with two other Parliamentary leaders, Colonels Poyer and Powell. This threat to the Parliamentarians was so serious that Oliver Cromwell himself led his troops to besiege Pembroke castle, and stayed in Carmarthen on the way. In July 1649 Cromwell again stayed at Carmarthen on his way to Ireland, lodging at the Nagg's Head in St Mary's Street.

The first few decades of the 18th century saw several changes taking place in the town. For example, in 1712 a fire engine was purchased, which must have been welcomed. In the same year a conduit brought a public water supply into the town from Waundew Common.

In 1723 £100 was spent on casting bells for St Peter's Church, and the Corporation agreed that the well and bathing house called Job's Well should be repaired for the benefit of the public. But it was not until the middle of the century that any major redevelopment took place in the town. Around 1765 the Tudor Guildhall, then in a very poor state, was demolished, and the Mayoral courts were removed temporarily to the Bumper Coffee Rooms. The meat shambles around the Guildhall moved to nearby Clos Mawr,

Conduit Lane

This lane runs alongside the foundations of the 1415 town wall; near here White Gate was constructed, following the Owain Glyn Dwr uprising. The lane is named after the site of a water supply brought into the town from Waundew Common. Note the wrought iron work above the lane, a link with Carmarthen's iron works.

CONDUIT LANE 2004 C31713k (Conrad Hughes)

and other stalls moved to the medieval Market Cross in Upper Market Street, now Nott Square. A temporary hall was erected, and although the borough mortgaged property and voluntary donations came flooding in, there was a long delay in the opening of the new Guildhall (53738), which did not take place until 1777 because of the Corporation's poor financial state. The situation was only saved by a gift of £4,000 from John Adams of Peterwell, Cardigan; he was subsequently elected MP for the borough. Today the Guildhall houses the County Council offices, the County Court, and the Magistrates' Courts and offices.

The Spilman Street Gate near St Peter's Church was removed in 1768 because the narrow-arched gateway was too small for wheeled vehicles such as stage coaches to enter and leave the town, or to go to the newly established iron and tin works. In 1792 White Gate was demolished, no doubt for the same reason. The Ivy Bush, a busy coaching Inn, in King Street - its arch is still visible - was very popular, and coaches would leave from an area called the Green, which later became the Green Post, a shop selling ladies' fashions. The busy road from the Quay to Guildhall Square, Quay Street, was paved and lowered in 1770. Quay Street had originated in the Norman town, and it became a busy thoroughfare for traffic taking goods from the quay to the town centre. During the 18th and 19th centuries wealthy merchants had houses here, and it became a fashionable quarter of town - note the fine examples of Regency houses in photograph C31715k. In 1777 the bridge was widened by six feet.

THE GUILDHALL 1893 53738

THE LOWER END OF QUAY STREET 2004 C31714k
(Conrad Hughes)

Originally this street was much longer than it is today, but in 1963 the bottom end was demolished for the construction of Coracle Way.

THE TOP END OF QUAY STREET 2004
C31715k (Conrad Hughes)

Thanks to public subscription, the Parade was constructed in 1782, giving the townspeople an excellent view of the Towy valley. In 1792 a new roof and ceiling was constructed at St Peter's Church by the architect John Nash, who also built a new county gaol after the last remains of the castle interior and prison had been cleared.

Did you know?

Before the building of the county gaol, prisoners were kept in the town goal situated above Prisoners Gate, between King Street and Nott Square. Prisoner debtors would lower down bags from the gate and beg for aid by shouting 'Remember the poor debtors.' Before 1818, public executions of convicts from the county took place at Pensarn, on the site of Capel Y Babell.

On 3 September 1792, the first meeting of the Carmarthen Commissioners of Paving and Lighting was held; this resulted in King Street being paved in 1793, with Dark Gate, Lammas Street, and Spilman Street all being paved by 1802. The Mayor, William Paxton, made plans to supply piped water throughout the town. The people of Carmarthen must have found these improvements an advantage.

A major step was undertaken in 1796 when the old medieval Wynveth Gate and nearby Cock Mill were removed and the Wynveth stream covered over to form a wagon road, now Blue Street, to the quay. This was to enable traffic to go directly from the quay to the new market, thus avoiding the congested Quay Street, Guildhall Square and Dark Gate. The new market opened in 1800 chiefly for the sale of meat, poultry and cheese.

Carmarthen was already a centre for the woollen industry, and in the 18th century it became the centre of the beaver and felt hat industry. A guild of hatters and felt-makers, the last of the guilds, was incorporated in

STORYBOARD SHOWING THE LOCATION OF DARK GATE 2004 C31716k (Conrad Hughes)

THE CROSSING, GUILDHALL SQUARE 1949 C31054

Lammas Street is straight ahead, with Blue Street to the left and Red Street to the right. Dark Gate in 1797 was called Union Place, and was located further into what is now Guildhall Square.

1651, paying £20 for the privilege. The tall beaver or steeple hat (36593) was a fashion seen in the larger towns like Carmarthen; it was made of hardboard with a thin layer of beaver felt glued to it. The origins of the Welsh hat and costume is unknown, but it would seem that the Welsh national costume of local striped and checked flannel is based on the common dress of the farm servants and cottagers worn in the 18th and 19th centuries. Old photographs of the town show Carmarthen people going about their daily tasks wearing national costume as late as the early 1900s.

PENSARN, WELSH COSTUMES 1895 36593

Note the glossy beaver hats! It would seem that the beaver hat was rather an expensive item, which prevented all but the well to do from wearing it, and would have been considered a luxury.

BEAVER HAT SIGN IN LAMMAS STREET 2004
C31717k (Conrad Hughes)

In Lammas Street, near the junction with Mansel Street, stood Masters, a gentlemen's outfitters who sold top hats. Today the sign is still there, but the shop now sells computers and office equipment.

As for the growth of industry in Carmarthen, iron and tin works were established in the mid 18th century on the north bank of the Towy, and to the east of the Old Priory; these industries flourished during the 19th century and employed a large labour force. Like every other iron works in the county, the Carmarthen iron works owes it origins to Robert Morgan. When he came to Carmarthen in 1748 he already owned several works. His earliest iron plants were sited in woodland areas, because charcoal was considered the best fuel to produce high grade pig-iron. The best timbers for smelting the iron were oak, which contained 23% charcoal, and elm, containing 19%. Rivers were important to the success of the industry. The Gwili, which ran into the Towy, provided an excellent water supply, whilst the iron ore could be brought into Carmarthen via the Towy, and the bark of the oak, considered ideal for tanning purposes, could be exported out of Carmarthen. In 1750 one hundred and fifty tons of iron bars were produced, rising to four hundred tons in 1788.

The tin mills gained an international reputation; all the products carried the mark 'M C' for Morgan of Carmarthen. Between 1777 and 1800 Robert Morgan's son John managed the business, and in 1792 to assist his business he established Furnace Bank, which issued its own coins and tokens (see below), which were payable in London, Bristol and Carmarthen. However, sometime before 1791 the town had its own first bank: this was David Parry's Bank, which was taken over by David Morris, a Carmarthen merchant of Dark Gate. He also took over John Morgan's Carmarthen Furnace Bank – later it was to become the National Provincial Bank, which in turn became the National Westminster Bank.

AN IRON WORKS HALFPENNY 2004
ZZZ00765 (Conrad Hughes)

This is a Carmarthen Towy works coin.

Furnace House

Furnace House in St Peter's Street was the home of the Morgan family; it was probably built by Robert Morgan in 1760. It is an excellent example of a Georgian town house. The preserved and restored façade features a raised porch with Corinthian pillars, and a forecourt enclosed within a wall. Each end of the wall is decorated with pineapple finials, and the iron gates and railings were cast at Robert Morgan's works. Note the lantern above the gate supported on iron pillars with the words 'M Busteed Fecit 1761' - M Busteed made it - cut into them. Legend tells us that Sir Thomas Picton dined here on 25 May 1815 before leaving for Waterloo; on leaving the house, he turned to Mr Morgan and said, 'Now for a peerage, or a glorious grave.' Today the County Library is housed here.

FURNACE HOUSE 2001 C31718k (Conrad Hughes)

THE PLAQUE ON FURNACE HOUSE 2004 C31719k (Conrad Hughes)

The 18th century saw a growth in political awareness, especially amongst the landed families, who were rivals under the banners Whig and Tory. Both parties encouraged bribery and corruption during elections, which in 1755 led to rioting and violence in the streets. During the early years of the century Carmarthen was mainly Whig, because on the death of Queen Anne in 1714, they supported George I. The Tories, because they supported an attempted Stuart restoration, were classed as Jacobite sympathisers and effectively kept out of office. In the 1741 election for Borough MP, John Philipps (a Tory) was elected through corrupt practices. He had been admitted as a burgess of

Carmarthen in 1737 and elected to the Council in 1738; he managed to influence the Council, and created about 200 new burgesses, most of whom came from neighbouring Pembrokeshire or from his own Tory supporters. The Tories now had a majority vote on the Council, but in the Borough Council elections the Whigs enlisted the support of the people of Carmarthen, who were dissatisfied at not having a voice in the administration of their own town. They rejected the Mayor and the two Sheriffs elected by the Tory Council, and proceeded to elect their own. Three years later the Whigs persuaded the Council to ban six of their Tory members; this resulted in Sir John Philipps being replaced by Griffith Philipps, who was supported by the local people. However, John Philipps and his Tory supporters continued on the Council side-by-side with the Whig Council, and for several years Carmarthen had two mayors, and on some occasions even three!

In the parliamentary elections of 1751 and 1754 Griffith Philipps was returned for Carmarthen, supported by local resident burgesses. The following year saw rioting in the streets, and several versions of what happened circulated - one from the Whigs, another from the Tories, and yet another reported by the tradesmen and merchants of the town. The Tory headquarters were at the Red Lion Inn in Guildhall Square, and the Whig headquarters at the Greyhound Inn in Bridge Street. According to the Whig Mayor, Evan Davies, five hundred people had come from Pembrokeshire and elsewhere with firearms; they were supported by the Sea Serjeants Club, a Jacobite club founded in south Wales – it flourished from about 1725 to 1764 to support the royal house of Stuart in exile. It was made up mainly of Tory squires; they met once a week in west Wales port or tidal towns to dine, entertain, and conduct meetings in private. The Society's secretary, John Philipps, and thirty-two of the Sea Serjeants were Tory burgesses in Carmarthen; all of them had been admitted when John Phillips gained power and created new burgesses. According to the tradesmen and merchants, the riots broke out when a crowd, armed with guns, swords and other weapons, assembled unlawfully and chased a number of inhabitants into the town hall. Essex Jones, a Sea Serjeant, fired a gun through one of the windows and wounded Jacob Morgan.

In December of that year the rioters regrouped; this time shots were fired into the open streets from the stables of the Red Lion Inn, resulting in two more deaths. The gatehouse between King Street and Nott Square continued to be garrisoned by an armed group of Red Lion people, who apparently fired at anyone they could.

In March 1756 the area was still occupied, and subsequently both the Whigs and the Tories took legal action against each other's supporters, but it seems that no one was punished for the rioting. The two parties continued to plot against each other, and to elect a Mayor each. A year later a further outbreak of violence erupted when a corn store was broken into: five rioters were killed, and the Mayor was tried and acquitted for murder. In 1763 the Whigs and the Tories

DARK GATE c1965 C31128

To the left is Blue Street, and to the right Red Street, scenes of bloodshed during the political battles of the 1770s. The hosiery store on the corner of Blue Street used to be the Naggs Head Tavern, which is mentioned in the rent roll of 1573. It was once owned by a Mr Bright who owned the Half Moon, a coaching inn next door, and in 1806 it became a bar and liquor store. Today, Red Street is a busy shopping centre.

both presented a petition to the Crown for a new charter favouring their own interests. However, in 1764 the Tory leader Sir John Phillips died, and in that year the Whigs gained a charter from King George III. It was brought to Carmarthen in August of that year and confirmed all the customs and privileges of former charters; it declared that there should be forty burgesses, and that one should be called Mayor. This period of unrest is remembered today in Red Lion Yard, which today is more of a passage leading from Guildhall Square to Chapel Street than a yard. In those days it was actually the rear of the Red Lion Inn, with the front facing Guildhall Square. Red Street takes its name from the colour of the Tory party, and Blue Street, which in 1797 was called Golden Grove Street, takes its name from the Whig party.

The Civil War years led to the growth of the Commonwealth Puritans. In Carmarthen they were mainly Independents and Baptists, who became the persecuted Dissenting Nonconformists during the Restoration period. Those who survived became the founding Welsh Nonconformists. This Nonconformism heralded the great religious revival of the 18th century, which also inspired the Methodist movement, which originated from a small group of Oxford students led by John Wesley and George Whitefield. After the dissolution of the monasteries and chantries, St Peter's Church remained the sole religious establishment in the town until 1726, when the first nonconformist August Street Chapel was built – it was replaced in 1826 by the chapel we see today (C31722k).

BLUE STREET 2004 C31720k (Conrad Hughes)

RED STREET 2004 C31721k (Conrad Hughes)

AUGUST STREET CHAPEL 2004
C31722k (Conrad Hughes)

Carmarthen's part in Calvinistic Methodism began with Peter Williams, a Methodist, revivalist and publisher of the Welsh Family Bible, known as Beibl Peter Williams in the 1770s. Whilst still a pupil at Carmarthen Grammar School, Peter converted to Methodism after listening to George Whitefield preaching in Lammas Street in 1743. The Welsh Calvinistic Methodists flourished, but the Wesleyan Methodists made limited progress despite John Wesley visiting Carmarthenshire at least fourteen times. He appeared to be happy to leave the Welsh-speaking area to the Welsh leaders, whilst he preached to the English speakers in the town. In 1763 he preached on the Castle Green, and the stone he is reputed to have stood on was later built into the wall of the Wesleyan Chapel in Chapel Street, which opened on 9 December 1804. The following year Carmarthen became the headquarters of the new Carmarthen Circuit, having previously been within the Haverfordwest Circuit. The chapel was enlarged in 1821, and rebuilt in the classical style in 1861 with the windows being incorporated into the Sunday school room. Finally the chapel was demolished in 1978 to make way for the new shopping centre. A new Wesleyan church was built-

THE WESLEYAN METHODIST CHURCH 2004
C31723k (Conrad Hughes)

with an old stone containing the words 'Wesleyan Chapel 1821' incorporated into the entrance of the new building beside a new stone (C31723k).

Penuel Chapel (C31724k, page 49), the oldest place of Baptist worship in Carmarthen, originated in a house in Old Chapel Yard, Priory Street (opposite the present chapel) in 1757, and here Stephen Davies preached. A baptismal service, which drew large crowds, was held in the River Towy in 1763. Interest in the movement increased, until in 1775 theological differences caused a rift. The more orthodox members under their ordained minister, the Rev David Evans, went to worship in nearby Priory Street, but in 1782 they moved to Eglwys y Porthtywl, an old mercantile house, in Dark Gate, where they remained until 1812. Tabernacle Chapel in Waterloo Terrace was built in the same year, thanks to the efforts of their minister Titus Lewis, who had unfortunately died the previous year, and never saw his new chapel. He is buried in the field on which the chapel was built. Thirty years later the chapel was rebuilt, and the schoolroom was rebuilt and enlarged in 1878. The old mercantile house was used as a monumental stone workshop during the 1900s; it was converted into offices in 1949 before finally being demolished in 1969 to make way for the modern shopping centre.

Other churches, too numerous to mention, grew up in the 19th century. Hand in hand with the religious revival went the Welsh educational movement, which began with Griffith Jones (1683-1761) of Llanddowror, founder of the circulating schools, which were run by itinerant schoolmasters who taught both children and adults to read the

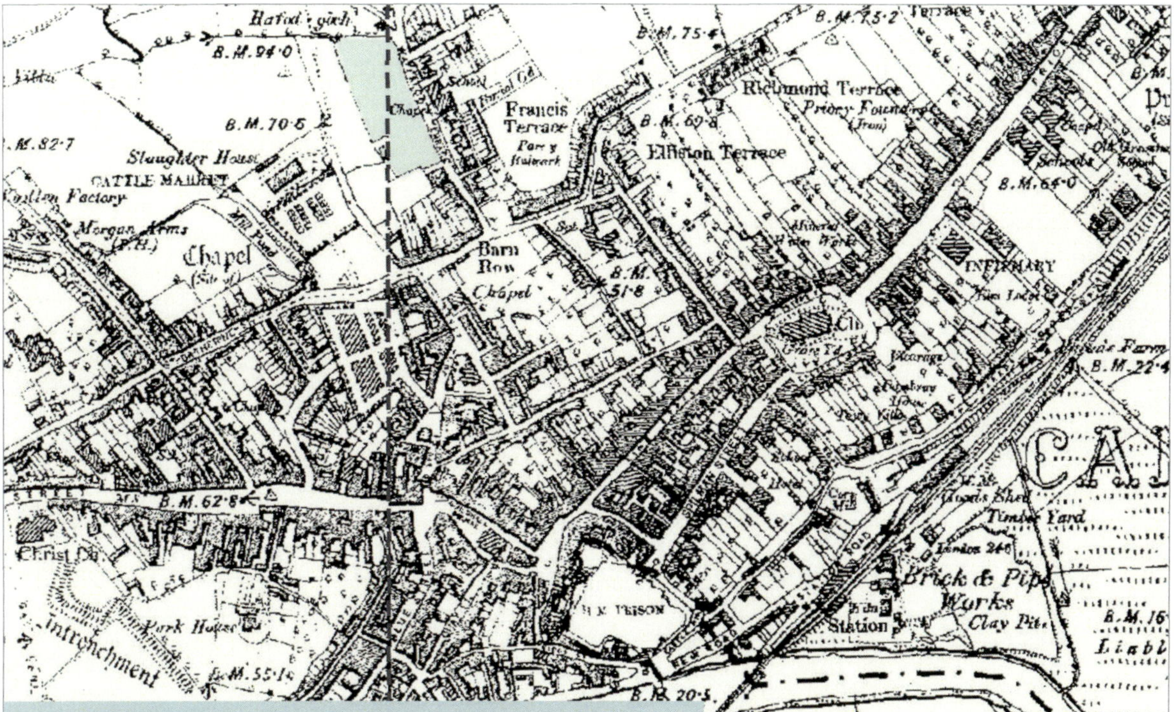

DETAIL OF CARMARTHEN ORDNANCE SURVEY MAP 1886

Detail of map showing the Tabernacle Terrace in Waterloo Road and the field in which it was built.

Welsh Bible. As the people learned to read, so their thirst for reading material grew, which led to the introduction of printing presses, and Carmarthen became the main centre of the Welsh book trade. The first printing press in Wales was set up in Newcastle Emlyn in 1718 by Isaac Carter. It was brought to Carmarthen in 1725, where a press had been started four years earlier by Nicholas Thomas, who was followed by John Breden in 1730. These three presses were the first in Wales.

PENUEL CHAPEL 2004 C31724k (Conrad Hughes)

Note the fine iron railing here, typical of those throughout Carmarthen, a reminder of a time when iron was produced in the town.

CHAPTER THREE

Poverty, Prosperity and Disorder

As the bells of St Peter's Church welcomed in the 19th century, little did the people of Carmarthen know that the town was about to enter a much needed era of expansion and prosperity, but one which would also bring it difficulties.

The long Napoleonic war had brought many of the farm workers into town, resulting in overcrowding, a shortage of food and a reduction of wages. Despite the poor conditions, there must have been great excitement in Carmarthen on 13 November 1805 when the coach arrived at the Ivy Bush Inn and the coachman brought the news that 23 days earlier the British fleet had destroyed the combined fleets of Spain and France at Cape Trafalgar. However, the cheering would have soon been tempered with sadness at the death of Admiral Lord Nelson, who only a year or two earlier had stayed with Lady Hamilton at the Ivy Bush, and had attended the theatre in King Street.

STEPS LEADING TO DAN-Y-BANC 2004
C31725k (Conrad Hughes)

Most of the town's 5,500 inhabitants were crowded into no more than 400 houses, huddled around the town's commercial area of Lammas Street, Guildhall Square, Upper Market Street (now Nott Square), King Street and Spilman Street. About two thirds of the men and women living in Priory Street were employed in the thriving iron and tinplate works, now a major employer, whilst the occupants of Catherine Street and Water Street found employment in the tanneries and woollen and paper mills that had sprung up around the town. A third of the population made a living from the river, and lived in a cluster of stone cottages in winding alleys that dropped down to a busy ship-lined quayside. Their neighbours were riverside labourers, known as hobblers, and two colonies of Cornish and Irishmen. The Irish had come to Wales to look for work following the potato famine, and had settled in one-roomed cottages, now demolished, in a lane called Dan-y-Banc (under the bank). The Cornishmen worked in the lead mines, and lived below the Irish in Towyside. The main route to this district was down steps from Castle Hill to Dan-y-banc (C31725k), which today are still in use.

Living conditions within the town were harsh, and many found solace in the vast number of pubs and gin houses in the town, which by 1829 amounted to 84! Little wonder family rows and brawls spilled out onto the streets, along with the odd intermittent mob rioting. One such event occurred on 25 September 1818 when the Carmarthen Mob, as they became known, gathered at the quayside to prevent butter and cheese from being exported whilst they went hungry. They boarded the ship and carried the goods back to the warehouse. Two days later another attempt was made to export the cheese, but again the mob took the goods back to the warehouse. The Carmarthen troop of Yeomanry and the Carmarthen Militia were called out, and finally the cheese left the port on 30 September. However, merchants took the hint, and decided that in future they would sell their products locally.

Despite these conditions, improvements were on the horizon. Some oil lamps were installed in 1800, with another fifty to come four years later. In September 1822 Carmarthen became one of the first towns in

THE RIVER TOWY AND THE BRIDGE 1910 62613

We know that a wooden bridge existed here in 1220, which may have been built by the Romans, but it was destroyed in 1233 and replaced by the seven-arched bridge we see here. The quayside was a very busy area, and it was from here that a dozen ships hooted in honour of Nelson's victory at Trafalgar.

Wales to be lit by gas when eighty public lamps and several shops were illuminated, and the Mayor and townspeople walked in procession through the streets in celebration. The Ivy Bush Hotel moved from King Street to Spilman Street in 1803, and by 1804 an important new road, Castle Hill, was constructed from the bridge to Spilman Street, allowing through traffic to by-pass the town centre. In the same year the quay was extended downstream, and by 1808-09 it was built up to the bridge.

The 1800s were a busy time for the port, with sail and steam vessels docking. There was also a thriving ship-building industry, particularly along the Pothouse bank to the west of Island Wharf, where ships of up to 300 tons, such as the 'Priscilla' (1806), the 'Albion' (1813) and the brig 'Hero' (1814) were built. Reports of up to 13 foreign vessels and 20 coast vessels are recorded as bringing in £3000 in duty. The first steam ship between Bristol and Carmarthen came into service in November 1830, and by March 1849 the journey took just 8 hours and 20 minutes. Imports included pickled herrings, which could be bought straight from the ship individually or by the barrel. The river played its part in leisure too, with cheap excursions, works outings and Sunday school outings to nearby Ferryside. But wherever there is a port there are smugglers, and the customs officers were kept busy. One story recalls that tipped-off customs men lay in ambush near the Royal Oak toll gate in Johnstown, but when they pounced on the smuggler he drove off past the Picton Monument with his cart full of illicit spirits, and delivered them safely at Llanarthney.

At 6pm on a warm evening in July 1865 the pleasure steamer 'Lily' was towed across the river and officially launched from the Pothouse as a band played from a nearby boat. The ship received a traditional Carmarthen welcome: throughout the day cannon echoed from the Pothouse, and other river boats sailed passed decorated with bunting, as a jubilant crowd celebrated in style. However, other than a small yacht for the Mayor in 1869, the ship building had now come to an end.

By 1831 the population had doubled to 10,000, mortality rates were high, and many families were reduced to destitution. Soup kitchens under the control of the Mayor and a local committee were set up and funded by public money to distribute food between January and March.

In an attempt to alleviate conditions, the Poor Law Amendment Act was passed in 1834, offering relief in Union Workhouses, although it was said that the rations given to prisoners in the town's goals were superior. Husbands, wives and children were separated, and overcrowding was common. Little wonder that the workhouse became a place to hate and fear – indeed, during the Rebecca Riots of 1843, the Union Workhouse was attacked.

Yet despite this, there was another side to Carmarthen. In previous centuries the port had connected Carmarthen to the outside world, and now from the 1830s the Ivy Bush and the Boar's Head hotels were busy

LAMMAS STREET 1949 C31068

accommodating coach passengers arriving from and leaving to all parts of the United Kingdom. Journeys were long and tedious, and overnight stays at coaching inns such as these were common. Photograph C31068 shows the Boar's Head hotel; from the 17th century this coaching inn had been busily accommodating travellers, and it was a venue for many balls held in the town. Opposite it, the Willow Café can be seen; here, visitors to Carmarthen in the next century would be served meals on blue and willow patterned china - hence the name.

THE BOARS HEAD HOTEL, LAMMAS STREET 2004
C31726k (Conrad Hughes)

Little has changed to the outside of the building since the early 19th century, and the narrow coach entrance is still visible.

> ## *Did you know?*
>
> *The Picton coach ran daily (except Sunday, a day of rest in Wales) to Swansea for a five and a half hour journey. The Paul Fry (a 4-inside post coach) left the Ivy Bush at 5am every morning except Sunday, and arrived in Cheltenham at 7pm the same evening. Passengers then had the option to leave immediately, arriving in London at 6am the next morning, or to spend a night at the Royal Hotel before departing at 8am the following morning. Other coaches, such as the Regulator and the Collegian, ran several days a week to different Welsh towns.*

Carmarthen's Assembly Rooms opened on 21 November, 1854, and played a major part in the social and cultural life of the town. Sometimes called the Public Rooms, they comprised a large hall seating 600 people and were licensed to stage plays. Both the Carmarthen Musical Society and the Choral Society had regular concerts, whilst visiting opera and drama companies were frequent visitors. The Assembly Rooms were used by the Carmarthen Literary and Scientific Institution, which provided a lending library, a reading room, a conversation room and rooms for games like chess and draughts.

What's on in Carmarthen

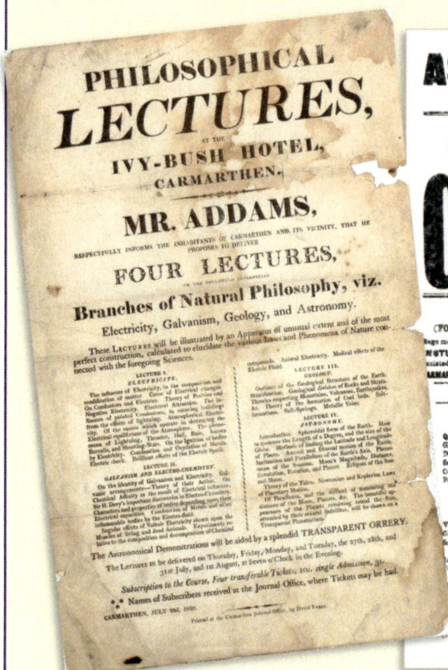

1.

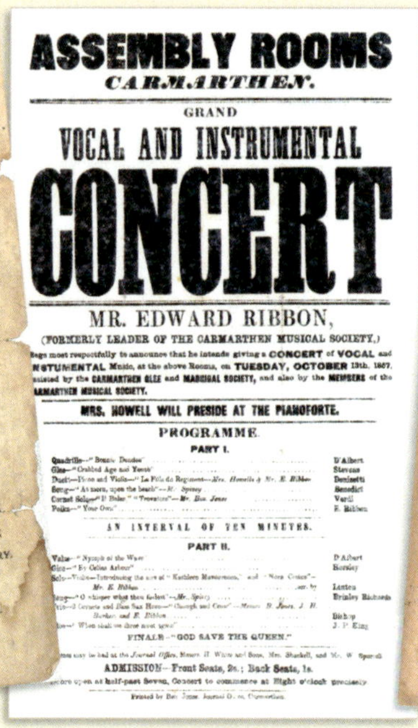

2.

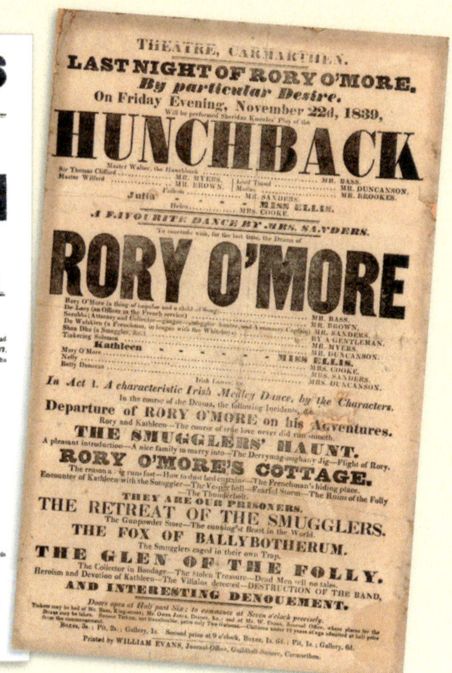

3.

Another attraction was the annual steeplechase, equivalent to today's point to point, so named because the rider had to aim at a church steeple or tower, and clear all the obstacles before racing to the finishing post. Race week was marked by two grand balls, one at the Ivy Bush Inn, the other at the Boar's Head, with usually four or five days being devoted to the racing. As early as 1801 the Corporation subscribed £25 towards the purchase of a plate to be awarded at the event.

The river played its part in fun and celebrations. Annual races for both large and small boats as well as coracles were held, and attracted many entries. Celebrations such as royal weddings and accession to the throne were marked with river races as well as by other sports in the town. On 10 March 1863, when Edward, Prince of Wales married Alexandra of Denmark, the day began with the town alive with the sounds of bells ringing and the firing of cannons, whilst everyone gathered in Guildhall Square at 11 o'clock. At mid-day a royal salute was fired, and a procession of the clubs, friendly societies and various churches paraded through the main streets, headed by their respective bands. Climbing the greasy pole took place in Nott-Square, Guildhall Square and Lammas Street, with legs of mutton offered as prizes. A ball was held in the newly built Assembly Rooms, and the day ended at 12 midnight with a large bonfire on Penlan Hill.

As far as law and order was concerned, Carmarthen had changed little since King Edward I gave the borough its first royal charter in 1285, together with a system called Watch and Ward, which meant twelve men patrolling the streets after a curfew. By the early part of the 19th century the town was watched over by Wil-y-Lon, Will the Lane; because he did the job on his own, he was given the nickname Will Alone. He had no uniform or a smart police station, but a windowless building known as the Roundhouse situated in Cambrian Place. Here he would lock up any prisoners to be brought before the magistrates the next day. The Roundhouse, erected in 1804, was continually used as a lock-up until about 1956, when a modern supermarket was built on the site.

1. IVY BUSH HOTEL POSTER FOR PHILOSOPHICAL LECTURES 1820 ZZZ00767 (Reproduced by kind permission of Carmarthenshire Records Office)

Mr Addams 'respectfully informs the inhabitants of Carmarthen and its vicinity that he proposes to deliver four lectures' on electricity, galvanism, geology and astronomy - Carmarthen was definitely a seat of learning.

2. ASSEMBLY ROOMS POSTER 1857 ZZZ00766 (Reproduced by kind permission of Carmarthenshire Records Office)

This poster advertises a vocal and instrumental concert. Front seats are advertised at 2 shillings, and would have been out of the reach of the poorer townspeople.

3. CARMARTHEN THEATRE POSTER ADVERTISING A SHERIDAN KNOWLES PLAY, 'RORY O'MORE' 1839 ZZZ00768 (Reproduced by kind permission of Carmarthenshire Records Office)

Because of gang riots, it was agreed that the borough magistrates would pay the constables for the lost wages due to injuries they received in suppressing a riot. They were not regarded as policemen as we know the term; rather, they were employed on an ad hoc basis, as in 1810 when men were engaged to supervise the fiftieth anniversary of the coronation of George III. The first mention of a Chief Constable occurs in 1827, when the Council appointed James Evans of Spilman Street on a salary of £20 a year. By 1857 the borough police force had reached a total of twelve - the twelve coppers - which affectionately became known as the Carmarthenshire Shilling!

A Tory, John Jones of Ystrad, after whom Johnstown is reputed to be named, became MP in 1821 and represented the borough until 1832. In March 1831 he voted against the Parliamentary Reform Bill, although he claimed he approved in principle. In the subsequent parliamentary elections the Carmarthen mob packed the Guildhall, threatening anyone who dared to vote for John Jones - the secret ballot was not introduced until 1872. Consequently the election was adjourned until the following day, but once again the mob stormed in intimidating the voters, and the election was cancelled. Thus Carmarthen entered the history books as the first town in Wales to have a parliamentary election prevented by pubic disorder. The Mayor and magistrates appealed to the Home Secretary for military help, and troops were dispatched from Brecon. However, fearing the consequences, the ringleaders gave themselves up and were jailed. With the town now quiet, the troops returned to Brecon and the trouble-makers were released on bail, but once they were released the mob rampaged through the streets.

A new election was fixed for 20 August 1831, and in anticipation of trouble six policemen from the newly formed London Metropolitan Police Force arrived in Carmarthen - one, John Lazenby, remained and was appointed Chief Constable. John Jones was duly elected, thanks to corrupt practices, and during his chairing ceremony in Guildhall Square he was pelted with stones. Several people were arrested, but violence continued for a few days before petering out. When the second Reform Bill was presented in September 1831, John Jones voted in favour of it to pacify the Carmarthen reformers, but the Bill was not passed, causing a national uproar; the third Parliamentary Reform Bill was finally passed in June 1832.

In 1833 'The Carmarthen Journal' reported further violence during council elections, and noted that the north and west galleries of the Guildhall were removed because they were used as vantage points for hurling missiles at the Sheriff and others. For many years the Borough of Carmarthen's affairs had been governed by corruption and negligence, with the result that Carmarthen owed over £2,000 to the bank. When the newly elected Council tried to obtain information from the last mayor regarding the accounts, his glib reply concluded with the lines:

'Do what you may, say what you will,
Asses will be but asses still.'

The Municipal Corporations Act of 1835 to reform town government proved no more beneficial for the town, and as a consequence discontent grew, leading to the Rebecca Riots. Although this was primarily a protest against the payment of tolls on the turnpike roads, the riots resulted from an accumulation of poverty and distress in the agricultural areas caused by poor harvests, a shortage of money, and high rents. Changes in the Poor Law Amendment Act of 1834 and conditions in the workhouses deterred people from seeking help; they preferred instead to live on the verge of starvation rather than give up their cottages, which would be seized by the landlord, and the furniture sold off to pay off debts.

Carmarthen was surrounded by five toll gates, but it was the Water Street Gate, kept by Henry Thomas, that caused the most anger. On 27 May 1843 he was woken from his sleep by 'Rebecca' and about three hundred of her 'children' on horseback, armed with axes, sledge hammers and guns. After Rebecca gave the order not to harm the Thomas family, they demolished the gate and made off into the hills. The gate was re-erected, but a few days later three men refused to pay the toll, and summonses were issued. They refused, probably because 'Rebecca' had threatened to burn their goods and kill them if they paid. Four constables were sent to arrest them, but were surrounded by around forty black-faced men armed with sticks and pitchforks, so the constables made a hasty retreat. Undeterred, the magistrates sent forty men, including regular armed police, specials, and army pensioners; they too were confronted by 'Rebecca' in full regalia, mounted on a white horse, accompanied by four hundred supporters. The police were pounced upon, and forced to march to the home of a leading county magistrate and made to demolish his boundary wall. Such defiance could not be tolerated, so the Mayor asked the Home Secretary to send troops to

The Rebecca Riots

During the late 1830s a network of unpopular toll-gates were erected in Wales, administered by Turnpike Trusts, who collected a toll – the money was supposedly to be used to improve the roads. They charged as much as a shilling for wagons and carts to pass through the tolls, which made farmers angry, especially when they had had a poor harvest. A group of men set themselves up as 'Rebecca and her daughters': with blackened faces and wearing women's clothing, they attacked the toll gates, destroying them by setting them alight. There were many 'Rebeccas', each leading his own group of men. The name Rebecca comes from the Bible, Genesis 24 verse 60: 'And they blessed Rebecca, and said unto her, Thou art our sister, be thou the mother of thousands of millions and let thy seed possess the gate of those which hate it.'

The Workhouse

THE WORKHOUSE 2004 ZZZ00787 (Reproduced by kind permission of David Jones, Cyhoeddiadau Cadno)
This photograph shows the western end of the building, which has been renovated and now accommodates the Learning Disabilities Team.

THE WORKHOUSE ENTRANCE 2004 C31727k (Reproduced by kind permission of David Jones, Cyhoeddiadau Cadno)
This is the entrance that was attacked in the 1843 riots. Today it is used by the Community Drugs Team.

THE PLAQUE COMMEMORATING THE 1843 RIOTS 2004 ZZZ00786 (Reproduced by kind permission of David Jones, Cyhoeddiadau Cadno)

Carmarthen. This request was quickly followed by another when it was discovered that 'Rebecca' had held a meeting of local farmers. The farmers had been ordered to meet on Monday 19 June 1843 at the Plough and Harrow, a public house two miles out of town, and march into Carmarthen.

That Monday a crowd of more than one thousand assembled outside the public house. 'Rebecca', wearing a horsehair wig of golden ringlets and mounted on a white horse, led the procession, while a band followed, playing popular songs of the day and carrying a banner with the inscription

'Cyfiawnder a Charwyr Cyfiawnder Ydym Ni Oll' (Justice, and lovers of justice are we all). The procession entered the Water Street Gate, while the Mayor and magistrates waited in Guildhall Square for the list of grievances to be presented. Suddenly the procession turned into Red Street and made towards the workhouse on Penlan Hill. Rebecca had lost control to the notorious Carmarthen mob! At the workhouse, Ray Evans, the master, was ordered to open the gates whilst the mob ransacked the building.

The Mayor sent the borough police and special constables to the workhouse to regain control. Meanwhile, Rebecca was confronted by the 4th Light Dragoons charging up Waterloo Terrace and Penlan Hill. The cavalry had been on their way to Carmarthen when they received news that the town was being invaded. One hundred rioters were taken prisoner, but only five were committed for trial at Carmarthenshire Assizes. A report from the Commission of Inquiry acknowledged the peoples' grievances, which resulted in all toll gates being removed. In 1848 Samuel Kentish was appointed Chief Constable, and although economic pressures continued, he brought stability to the borough.

Carmarthen has a rich Victorian heritage of schools, colleges, hospitals and other institutions. The foundation stone of the first training college in Wales to train teachers for the Welsh charity schools systems, founded as the South Wales and Monmouthshire Training College (53735), was laid on 16 July 1847 by Connop Thirlwall, Bishop of St David's. The day was declared a public holiday for the people of Carmarthen, and the shops were closed, so that the townspeople could join the mile-long procession from the Guildhall to the college.

THE TRAINING COLLEGE 1906 53735

The Girls' Grammar School

10 QUAY STREET 2004
C31730k (Conrad Hughes)

PLAQUE ON THE GIRLS' GRAMMAR SCHOOL 2004 C31731k (Conrad Hughes)

The formal opening of the college took place on 24 October 1848, and was marked by a service in St Peter's Church attended by the Mayor. The college came into being largely through the influence of Bishop Thirlwall, with strong support from the Welsh Education Committee of the National Society. The first principal was Canon William Reed; the college opened with 28 Anglican male students, with an intake of 49 the following year.

At this time plans were being made to open three model schools for boys, girls, and infants - but lack of funds meant that only the Model School for Boys was opened in 1849. The Girls' Model School did open two years later. The first division paid 3d a week, and were taught to write in copy books. Division 2 paid 2d a week; they were taught fewer subjects, and used slates to write on.

The Girls' Grammar School was founded in September 1895 as the Carmarthen County Girls' School. It opened at a town house, 10 Quay Street (C31730k). It began with 35 pupils, but by 1888 numbers had increased to 80.The school was officially named the County Girls' School, but for many years was known as the Intermediate School, or 'the 'Inter'. In 1899 the school moved to new premises adjacent to the Boys' Grammar School between Richmond Terrace and Wellfield Street, a new purpose-built building in Wellfield Road, but many of the girls who had been in the Quay Street premises did not like the change. The school in Quay Street had a family feel to it, but in the larger building the pupils felt isolated and school life seemed too formal.

THE OLD COLLEGE OF ART 2004
C31732k (Conrad Hughes)

The Carmarthen School of Art, the first of its kind in Wales, was founded in Parade Road in 1854. When it outgrew the building, a new school was built in Church Lane, opposite St Peter's Church (C31732k), with money coming from public subscriptions. 'Ye Fancye Fair' was held in the Market Place in July 1891, which raised £480 towards the red brick building; it opened on 22 September 1892 with accommodation for 70 students. Today, it houses the Oriel Gallery.

To cope with the social needs of the day and the expanding community, it was agreed to open an infirmary at the barracks on Picton Terrace, but when the old borough goal was offered rent free, the hospital started there with 12 patients. Numbers rapidly increased in 1849 to 78 inpatients and 542 outpatients receiving treatment. However, in 1847 a decision was taken to build an infirmary on the site of the old Grammar School in Priory Street. A tender for £3260 was accepted from the contractor William Lewis, and the money was to be found by public subscription. Every week the Carmarthen journal reported on donations, and when the Lyric theatre reopened, the first night's takings were given to the fund. Bishop Connop Thirlwall laid the foundation stone on May 1857. The hospital opened on 1 July 1858 in a building that could accommodate 30-40 patients (77291). It is an interesting fact that donations kept the hospital going until the advent of the National Health Service in 1948. The hospital continued as a maternity and geriatric hospital (part of West Wales Hospital, Glangwili) until 1966. Today the building is being converted into flats; the first residents are due to move in shortly.

Did you know?

The West Wales Hospital at Glangwili started life as a collection of Nissen huts, which had been constructed to provide hospital accommodation for the American army during the Second World War. In fact, the casualties did not materialise, and the huts were turned into a prisoner-of-war camp, surrounded by barbed wire. After the war the huts were gradually replaced with the present buildings. Today the modern hospital serves the county of Carmarthenshire.

THE WAR MEMORIAL AND THE INFIRMARY 1925 77291

In 1865 St David's Mental Hospital opened as the Joint Counties Lunatic Asylum serving Carmarthenshire, Cardiganshire and Pembrokeshire.

It was originally built by Mr Pollard of Taunton to hold 600 patients, officers and staff; it was enlarged in 1895 to accommodate a new female hospital, a hospital for infectious diseases, and a new chapel with seating for 500 people (41095, see page 65). At this date there were 286 male and 271 female patients. All the stone was quarried, and all the work carried out, by the staff and patients to a design by a local architect, Ernest Collier. The hospital is due to close some time this year (2004).

THE ASYLUM 1898 41095

ST DAVID'S HOSPITAL FROM THE AIR 2004 ZZZ00769 (Reproduced by kind permission of David Jones, Cyhoeddiadau Cadno)

The first railway train arrived in Carmarthen on 6 September 1852, although it only carried material for the line and not passengers. Everyone who turned out to watch looked on in horror as it 'raced' into the station at 15 mph! However, the official opening took place almost two weeks later on 17 September, when three trains left Swansea complete with officials and a military band, which played at each station along the line.

Carmarthen station was situated about one mile outside the town at Myrtle Hill, Pensarn. Initially five trains a day ran in each direction on the single line, and more ran when the second track was introduced four months later. London was now only ten and a half hours away! Just over a year later the line was extended westwards to Haverfordwest; the line crossed the River Towy by way of an iron bridge, which was hinged to allow the ships to pass.

In 1857 the Carmarthen & Cardigan Company began work on a line to Cardigan, but it was not until March 1860 that the first mile was completed and a new town station opened at Kidwelly Fach, below the Parade. After spending over half a million pounds and liabilities of a million, the line still only reached Llandyssul, and in November 1864 a receiver was appointed. However, the company limped on until 1888, when it was bought by the GWR.

THE BRIDGE c1950 C31004

The iron bridge spanning the river Towy was built in 1858 to carry the railway from Myrtle Hill Junction to the station, then on to Llandeilo and central Wales. Passenger traffic ceased on this line in 1965 and freight traffic in 1973.

THE 'CARMARTHEN CASTLE' LOCOMOTIVE NAMEPLATE 2004
ZZZ00771 (Conrad Hughes. Reproduced by kind permission of Carmarthen Town Council)

The 'Carmarthen Castle' locomotive was built in February 1924 and began its life operating from Old Oak Common, outside London Paddington. It ended its days in Llanelli, and was withdrawn in February 1963. This nameplate hangs in St Peter's Civic Centre.

Gentleman's Ticket.
Opening of the South Wales Railway
to
Carmarthen.
Admit the Bearer to the
Public Breakfast at two o'Clock on
the 17 day of September 1852.
No. 701.

A GENTLEMAN'S TICKET FOR THE OPENING OF THE RAILWAY 1852 ZZZ00770 (Reproduced by kind permission of Carmarthenshire Records Office)

The 19th century saw the erection of several monuments and plaques in Carmarthen. The first was erected in memory of General Sir Thomas Picton, who was killed at the Battle of Waterloo on 18 June 1815. The original monument was designed by John Nash, and was built by local stonemason David Mainwaring. It stood 75 ft high; an internal winding staircase led to the column, where there was a square gallery with cannons placed in each corner. The monument was decorated with bas-relief scenes depicting Picton's triumphs. It cost £3,000 to build from public subscription. The monument was dedicated on 29 July 1828, but within a few years the bas-reliefs suffered in Carmarthen's climate. Replacement carvings were made by the original sculptor, Edward Hodges Baily, but they were never erected, and lay neglected and forgotten until they were discovered in a garden in 1970. In 1846 the monument was taken down, and the foundations for the second monument (C31117) were laid in 1847. However, this monument was struck by lightning in 1854, and the top had to be removed.

The Royal Welch Fusiliers Monument in Lammas Street (32781) was erected in 1858 in memory of the men of the 23rd Royal Welch Fusiliers who died in the Crimean War in 1854-55. Fine cast iron railings in the form of crossed muskets were placed around the monument, and a Russian cannon brought from the Crimea was placed in front of the

The Picton Monument

THE PICTON MEMORIAL 1959 C31117 (above)

THE PICTON MONUMENT 2004
C31733k (Conrad Hughes) (left)

In 1988 the Picton monument was rebuilt on stronger foundations, and during this process a 'time capsule' containing Picton's Waterloo medal and a selection of 1799-1825 coins were found. When the monument was restored, a full set of 1988 coins and plaque of the coat of arms of Carmarthen District Council were placed under the foundations.

monument, but this was melted down during the Second World War for scrap to aid the war effort. The cannon, and stones placed around the monument to prevent carriage wheels from knocking against it, are visible in photograph 32781.

The Nott Monument (77289, C31734k), erected in March 1851 on the site of the covered market place, commemorates Carmarthen's most famous son, General Sir William Nott, son of Charles Nott, once proprietor of the Ivy Bush in King Street. The monument, to which Queen

LAMMAS STREET 1893 32781

Did you know?

The 23rd Royal Welch Fusiliers were founded by William III (William of Orange) to oppose James II in 1689. It is claimed that the first man to join the Fusiliers came from Friars Park in Carmarthen.

Victoria contributed 200 guineas, is the work of the sculptor Edward Davis, son of Dr David Davis of Llandyfaelog (he became a famous London physician and attended the birth of Queen Victoria). The bronze statue was cast from guns captured at the Battle of Maharajur, which were presented by the East India Company. Sir William had a distinguished career in India and Afghanistan and returned home to Job's Well in Johnstown. He died in January 1854, and was buried in St Peter's churchyard, near to his parents.

South Wales Daily News
VESTERN MAIL
ANGEL VAULTS.
ALLSOPP'S
EMPIRE
ALES.
NOTT

THE NOTT MONUMENT 1925 77289

THE NOTT MONUMENT, NOTT SQUARE 2004
C31734k (Conrad Hughes)

Until the mid 1850s Carmarthen continued to be the most populated town in Wales, until the industrialised towns of Llanelli and Swansea overtook it; this was because most of the industrial businesses in Carmarthen were service industries for agriculture. The one exception was the Morgan family's iron and tin businesses - these were the biggest employers in the town until they closed in 1900, a severe blow.

The beginning of the 19th century saw the founding of some well-known and interesting local businesses. For example, David Brigstocke ran a well-respected painting, decorating, paper-hanging and glazier's business from 61 King Street – his firm painted and decorated the Guildhall in 1805. His sons were also well known in the town: John Lewis Brigstocke became a printer, and Charles Brigstocke was a wine merchant in St Peter's Street. Charles's son James established a pharmacy at 25 King Street in 1869 (C31735k) - he was the first qualified chemist and druggist in the town. James became well known far and wide for his Carmarthen Balsamic Cough Linctus, renowned to cure coughs, colds and even whooping cough! He also provided cattle and sheep dips, veterinary ointments, and liniments of every description, gaining the confidence of local medical practitioners as well as cattle breeders, farmers and the general public. The business was subsequently acquired by D King Morgan at the beginning of the 20th century, and still serves the townspeople today.

Another of David Brigstocke's sons, Thomas, was educated at the Queen Elizabeth Grammar School, but at sixteen he was sent to the academy of a Mr Sass RA, in Bloomsbury in London, where he studied before becoming an accomplished artist.

THE PHARMACY, 25 KING STREET 2004 C31735k
(Conrad Hughes)

Note the large apothecary bottle in the window.

The Emporium

A shop called the Emporium was the most ornate Victorian building in the town with its distinctive five arches supported by six classical columns. It can be seen in this photograph on the left-hand side past the lamppost. The business was founded by Henry Thomas in the 1880s and provided quality goods for the townspeople, such as carpets, lino, curtains and bedding. It also had a department selling gentlemen's clothes, hosiery, scarves and gloves. A central staircase led to a dress-making and millinery department on the first floor, and some of the staff of 30 female assistants, errand boys and delivery men were accommodated in bedrooms on the top floor. The building was pulled down in 1954, and the famous façade was replaced by glass windows.

THE EMPORIUM 1893 32780 (detail of larger print)

THE COFFEE POT 2004 C31737k (Conrad Hughes)

The 1975 Coffee Pot seen here was refurbished in 1992 by Gwyn Phillips and encased in fibreglass for protection.

ADVERTISEMENT FOR WONNACOTT'S TEA WAREHOUSE, 'CARMARTHEN JOURNAL' 1855 ZZZ00785

(Reproduced by kind permission of Carmarthen Library)

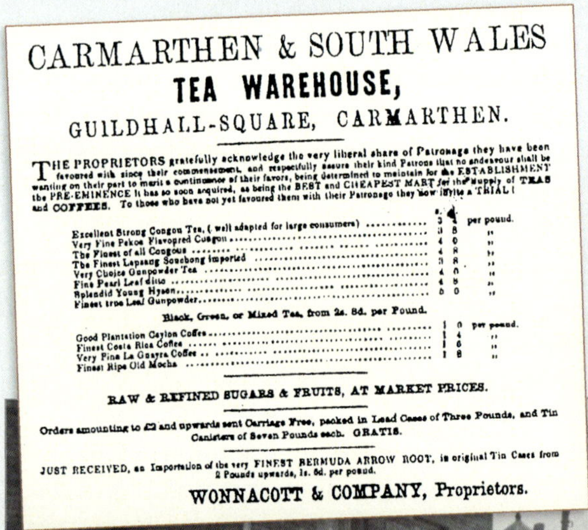

CARMARTHEN & SOUTH WALES

TEA WAREHOUSE,

GUILDHALL-SQUARE, CARMARTHEN.

THE PROPRIETORS gratefully acknowledge the very liberal share of Patronage they have been favoured with since their commencement, and respectfully assure their kind Patrons that no endeavour shall be wanting on their part to merit a continuance of their favors, being determined to maintain for the ESTABLISHMENT the PRE-EMINENCE it has so soon acquired, as being the BEST and CHEAPEST MART for the supply of TEAS and COFFEES. To those who have not yet favoured them with their Patronage they now invite a TRIAL!

	s.	d.	
Excellent Strong Congou Tea, (well adapted for large consumers)	3	4	per pound.
Very Fine Pekoe Flavoured Congou	3	8	,,
The Finest of all Congous	4	0	,,
The Finest Lapsang Souchong imported	4	8	,,
Very Choice Gunpowder Tea	3	8	,,
Fine Pearl Leaf ditto	4	0	,,
Splendid Young Hyson	4	8	,,
Finest true Leaf Gunpowder	5	0	,,

Black, Green, or Mixed Tea, from 2s. 8d. per Pound.

Good Plantation Ceylon Coffee	1	0	per pound.
Finest Costa Rica Coffee	1	4	,,
Very Fine La Guayra Coffee	1	6	,,
Finest Ripe Old Mocha	1	8	,,

RAW & REFINED SUGARS & FRUITS, AT MARKET PRICES.

Orders amounting to £2 and upwards sent Carriage Free, packed in Lead Cases of Three Pounds, and Tin Canisters of Seven Pounds each. GRATIS.

JUST RECEIVED, an Importation of the very FINEST BERMUDA ARROW ROOT, in original Tin Cases from 2 Pounds upwards, 1s. 6d. per pound.

WONNACOTT & COMPANY, Proprietors.

GUILDHALL SQUARE 1949 C31072

At the corner of Dark Gate and Guildhall Square was Wonacott's Tea and Coffee Warehouse. It can be identified by a coffee pot (C31072, C31737k), which was mentioned in a poem circulating around 1856:

'When first I was set up on high,
Some viewed me with a jealous eye,
With thoughts that I, an empty pot,
Would custom bring to Wonacott.'

According to research undertaken by Mrs Edna Dale-Jones, a well-known local historian, and published in an article in The Carmarthenshire Antiquary in 2002, the story surrounding the coffee pot is thus: In 1907 George Eyre Evans, Secretary of the Carmarthenshire Antiquarian Society, published the verse and asked who the author was. Mr Charles Finch, who ran a fishmonger's in Nott Square, lent or gave a copy of a book, 'Poetical Pieces' (subtitled 'Moral and Satirical Pieces'), to the Society's library. The book, which is now in Carmarthen Museum, contains 33 poems including the one above; it was written by Alexander Aitkin, and published in 1856. It would appear that three pots have hung on the corner of the building. The original was made some time before 1856; the second was made between 1871 and 1883, and was constructed of wood by D M Williams; and a third, also in wood, was made by Ryan Joinery in 1975.

At the end of the century William Spurrell died. He was best known for his book 'Carmarthen and its Neighbourhood', which was first published in 1860 - it was the first record of the town's history and contemporary events. Spurrell was born in Quay Street in 1813, and became one of the best-known printers, Welsh scholars, and local historians of his time. He was educated at Queen Elizabeth Grammar School, and at the age of 16, became apprenticed to John Powell Davies, a printing firm in King Street. After five years he went to Bradbury & Evans in London, where he worked on the first editions of Charles Dickens's novels 'Pickwick Papers' and 'Nicholas Nickleby', as well as Disraeli's 'Henrietta Temple'. When he returned to Carmarthen in 1839 he established his own business in Lower Market Street in 1840, before moving to 37 King Street, where it remained for nearly a hundred years. At a time when the Welsh language was being discriminated against, Spurrell produced the first edition of the Welsh-English Dictionary in 1848, and the English-Welsh dictionary in 1850, as well as Welsh Grammar Lesson in Welsh, and an English-Welsh primer. He died in 1899, and is buried in St David's churchyard.

PLAQUE IN KING STREET IN MEMORY OF WILLIAM SPURRELL 2004 C31738k (Conrad Hughes)

FILL HERE
ESSO
ETHYL

CHAPTER FOUR

Into the 20th Century with Pride

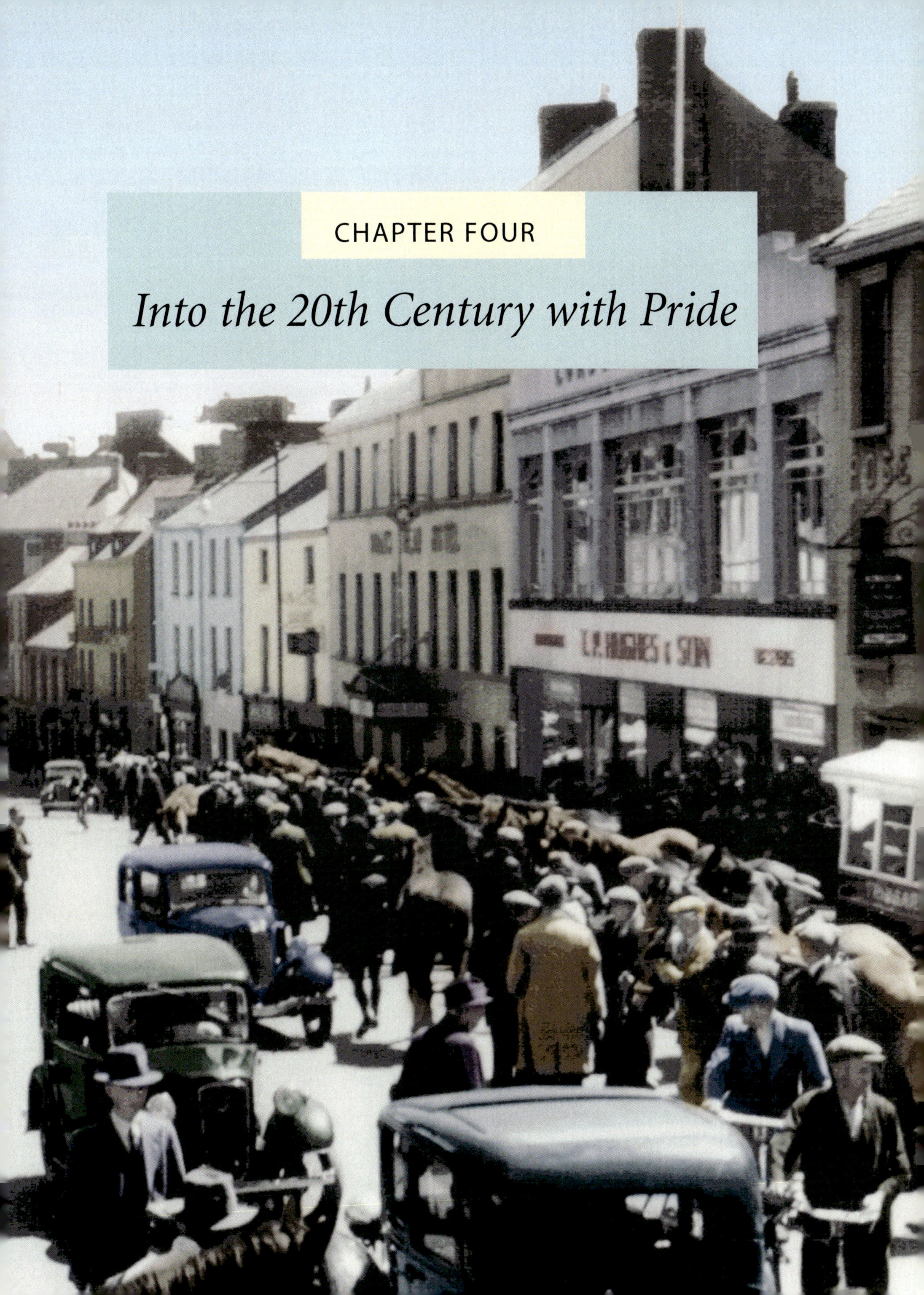

THE PARK, THE BANDSTAND 1949 C31062

ONE OF the big attractions for 20th-century Carmarthen must have been the opening on Easter Monday of Carmarthen Park, which featured a bandstand, a rugby pitch, and a 'magnificent cycle track of cement that is said to rival any track in England or Wales' (62618). 'The Carmarthen Journal' reported that it had been built 'with a view of attracting visitors to the town to witness cycle races and other sports', which must have pleased D Bradbury Jones, who kept the Leader Cycle and Motor Works opposite the post office in King Street. He sold a bicycle called the Bradbury, as well as the celebrated Leader motorcycle.

The park became a popular venue not only

Shops in King Street

It was at No 51 King Street, on the left-hand side of the picture, where Bradbury's sold cycles. On the junction of Queen Street and King Street we see the Anchor Café, a popular meeting place, where high-class fancy cakes and chocolate were sold. The shop was once owned by Thomas Henry, and was then called the Golden Anchor, a drapery and millinery shop. When he opened the Emporium mentioned in Chapter 3, the name remained. Another Emporium stood opposite at numbers 1,2 and 3, which around 1883 became the Cloth Hall - hence the sheep sign hanging above (right), a further reminder of the town's woollen trade.

KING STREET 1925 77285

THE RECREATION GROUND 1910 62618

This photograph shows the magnificent concrete cycle track.

for sports meetings, but also for circus trapeze artists, and the American trick cyclist Schreyer attracted a huge crowd on Whit Monday 1905. Carmarthen had always been a sporting town, and from as early as 1877 annual sports and bicycle races organised by Carmarthen Athletic Sports Club took place at the Mansel Athletic ground, a field near Picton's monument. Events included running, hurdles, walking, cycling, and sack races, tug-of-war and pony trotting.

Cycle races would start in John Street, with competitors racing down Catherine Street, around the monument, and down Lammas Street, to finish in front of the Guildhall. These races became so popular that competitors travelled from as far afield as Bristol and Cardiff, no doubt attracted by the prize of £3 for a 100-yard foot race, and 20 guineas for a one-mile race.

The park was used during the Proclamation ceremony of the National Eisteddfod in 1910, and again for the National Eisteddfod in 1911, when a temporary pavilion was erected. (Note the oak tree to the left of picture 62619, page 82, which formed the centre of the Gorsedd Circle in the 1910 Proclamation ceremony and also the Eisteddfod in 1911). Although it rained every day, the newspapers reported that this did not stop the crowds from enjoying themselves. During Eisteddfod week a plaque was placed on the wall of the house in which Brinley Richards the composer was born. Together with John Ceiriog Hughes the lyric writer, he wrote the anthem 'God Bless the Prince of Wales'.

The unveiling of the Boar War Monument in front of the Guildhall on 27 April 1906 by Major General MacKinnon would have drawn a large crowd, especially as its erection was promoted by 'The Carmarthen Journal'. The contractors were John Lewis & Sons, the marble masons, and one of the architects was Ernest Vale Collier, who helped to amass the museum's collection of early Roman coins. An architect by trade, he was also a talented artist; he served on the Borough Council from 1906 to 1921, and he was director of the Carmarthenshire Antiquarian Society and Field Club from 1920-32, during which time he never missed a field trip. The society was founded in April 1905 and promoted the study, collection and conservation of the county's history and archaeology. Each week it published a column of notes, articles and reports of researches in the Welshman, a newspaper with offices located in Lammas Street. In 1944 the Welshman ceased publication, and its title was acquired by its rival, 'The Carmarthen Journal'. Over the next forty years just fifty copies were produced each week, until finally in 1984 the title could not continue - it was incorporated into the 'Journal'.

'God Bless the Prince of Wales'

Whilst adjudicating at the National Eisteddfod held at Caernarvon Castle in 1862, Brinley Richards met John Ceiriog Hughes, a well-known poetry writer. At the time there were rumours that the then Prince of Wales, Prince Albert Edward, was to announce his marriage to Princess Alexandra of Denmark, so they decided to write a special anthem together. Ceiriog supplied the words and Brinley composed the tune. The anthem was first performed in January 1863 to coincide with the announcement of the royal engagement. The royal wedding in March 1863 ensured its success when the press referred to it as 'the Prince of Wales Anthem', and 'our Second National Anthem'. Just before Brinley died in 1885 at the age of sixty-seven, he wrote the following words: 'There is a glorious future for Wales; with such charming melodies Wales ought, and will, one day take a prominent position in the world of art.'

HALL STREET, PLAQUE COMMEMORATING BRINLEY RICHARDS 2004 C31739k (Conrad Hughes)

The Spencer Brothers and their Air Balloon

Two years before this photograph was taken, the Spencer brothers from London brought an 80ft air balloon to Carmarthen, planning to fly in the bamboo box attached to it. Thousands gathered to watch, but just before it was due to take-off at 4pm, a rip in the silk balloon was discovered. Two women came to the rescue and stitched it up, and finally at 7pm it rose into the air carrying the brothers – but by then many spectators had left to catch trains and buses home.

THE RECREATION GROUND 1910 62619

Did you know?

The quayside area of the town saw the erection of the Western Counties Agricultural warehouse (WCA), built in 1904 to a French design (62615, C31057). This was one of the earliest reinforced concrete buildings in the country; it remained in use until it was demolished in 1979.

THE RIVER TOWY FROM THE BRIDGE 1910 62615

FROM RIVERSIDE WALK 1947 C31057

THE CAPITOL, JOHN STREET 2004
C31740k (Conrad Hughes)

THE LYRIC THEATRE, KING STREET 2004
C31741k (Conrad Hughes)

With a new century came the advent of silent films. Carmarthen was later than most towns to establish a permanent cinema, but by 1914 there were two cinemas. The Rink Picture House in Old Station Road was so named because the building originally housed a roller-skating rink; it opened in 1909 when skating became a nationwide craze. Skating never took off in Carmarthen, and the building was soon turned into a cinema holding 700 people. The other cinema in Blue Street, owned by Mr Leon Vint, became known as Vint's Electric Palace. It opened on 1 April 1912 with seating for 600, and was advertised as having 'modern' electrical heating, ventilation and plumbing! It had a short life as a cinema and closed in April 1914, only to open a week later as the Empire Theatre with its own orchestra. It closed in the 1930s, and became the Oscar Chess Garage. The main part of the Assembly Rooms situated in King Street was also converted into a concert hall and cinema called the Lyric; it opened in March 1918 with the film 'Rasputin'.

Talking films came to Carmarthen in March 1930 when the Lyric put on 'Sonny Boy' featuring Al Jolson, whilst in August the Capitol cinema opened with 'Desert Song'. The Capitol (C31740k) was built on the site of the old tannery in John Street at a cost of £10,000, and boasted seating for 800. The Capitol was always used for the weigh-ins for the boxing shows that took place in Carmarthen market during the 1960s, when famous boxing champions like Howard Winstone, Dick Richardson and Brian Curvis boxed. It was later converted into a bingo and snooker hall, and today it is a health club.

LAMMAS STREET c1950 C31032

Lammas Street is the widest street in the town, making it easy for the coaches arriving at the Boars Head in the last century to turn

The Lyric was rebuilt again using a design by the architect William S Wort of Cardiff, and included luxurious seating for 1,000 people; it had excellent acoustics. On 6 April 1936 it reopened as the Lyric Theatre with Richard Tauber in 'Heart's Desire', but like many cinemas it could not compete with television, so it eventually closed. However, in recent years, thanks to dedicated work by Carmarthen Youth Opera and financial assistance from the local authorities, it once more opened as a theatre, cinema and concert hall (C31741k). In 1988 the building was taken over by the Lyric Theatre Trust (Carmarthen) Ltd, and it is run by a small staff and volunteers.

With the introduction of the motor car the town saw several businesses taking advantage of the times. John Bowen & Sons ran a hardware business in Lammas Street (77287, left); here all sorts of goods were displayed and sold. The shop extended back towards the old Friary. Nails were sold by weight, along with iron bars of varying widths, and rope of all thickness hung from the rafters. Now the business sold Shell petrol from hand pumps, and John Bowen looked after his favoured customers by allowing them to park their cars on his premises on market days. However, the agricultural strand was not forgotten; John Bowen's were the agents for Fordson tractors. Across the road at number 15, the Rees family ran the Angel Motors Garage on the site of the Angel, an old coaching inn. Photograph C31032 shows the two garages, with the Esso sign clearly visible on the right.

LAMMAS STREET 1925 77287

John Bowen's shop is to the left. Outside are milk churns, hen-coops and water barrels, whilst around the shop is a variety of garden tools, pitch forks and wooden rakes. A few doors up from this shop is the Drovers Arms.

Traditionally a market town, Carmarthen had held cattle markets, horse fairs and hiring fairs since medieval times, and a glance at Kelly's Directory for 1923 reveals just how many took place. In that year cattle fairs were held over two days in March, April, June and November, with one-day fairs in July, August and September. The advent of the motor car must have created a problem for farmers trying to conduct business in the streets. We learn from 'The Carmarthen Journal' that in June 1910, 150 horses including 50 colts had blocked the pavements and caused damage to windows - perhaps the animals were seeking refuge from the cars. Finally the police agreed that in future, horses would not be allowed on the pavement. The following month, the newspaper reported that the fair held in Priory Street had not been a large one, with insufficient stock to satisfy the needs of the buyers. We can only surmise that the cars had deterred some sellers from attending. Cars would certainly have had second place in Lammas Street on fair days (C31085). Shops would have reported a brisk trade during the fairs, and stores like TP Hughes & Sons at London House (C31085, right) would have sold household linen, carpets, furniture, and material for made-to-measure curtains.

THE HORSE FAIR c1940 C31085

Carmarthen's November fair, one of the highlights of the year, was held opposite the cattle mart, hence the name Fair Lane. It took place around 14 November, after harvesting, the end of the year for farm hands and maids, so the fair came as a welcome relief from hard work. Those who were not completely satisfied with their employers would look for a change of employment and possibly a higher wage. As late as the 1920s, farm lads were offered an annual wage of £10 or £15, not a great deal for the work involved. Free time was limited, but Sunday evening was always free so that the hands could attend chapel or church. These fairs must have been the equivalent to a trip to Disneyland today for these workers, where they would enjoy the shooting galleries or the coconut shy. The highlight for the children would have been the chip cart with its distinctive smell of frying fat, and the excitement of eating chips from a cone of greaseproof wrapped in a square of newspaper. The older men would end up at one of the many public houses in the town, whilst the women would go home clutching a pot of homemade pickle or jam, and some kippers or bloaters, which they would cook on a long iron tong, an indoor barbecue of the 20s.

THE DROVERS ARMS, LAMMAS STREET 2004 C31742k
(Conrad Hughes)

The Drovers Arms stands opposite the Boar's Head Hotel, a reminder of the days when this wide street would have been full of livestock.

Until the 1960s, Carmarthen on cattle mart days was like a scene from a Wild West film as cattle bought at the mart were herded along Richmond Terrace, up Little Water Street, into King Street and down to the cattle pens at the old station. Their ultimate destination was the dining tables of homes in England. The town would have been alive with the sound of thundering hooves and the lowing of the cattle, whilst terrified children clutched their mother's hands, and the occupants of Little Water Street pressed themselves against the walls so as not to be crushed against the walls of the terraced houses in the narrow street. However, there was little opposition to the marts, as traders would report good business - farmers with pockets full of money were willing to spend.

Did you know?

The trade in geese would take place at the goose fair, and once purchased the feet of the geese would be prepared for the long journeys, sometimes as far as the Midlands, by first making the birds walk over pitch or tar and then over fine sand. One of the main streets in Carmarthen was once called Goose Lane, and quite near the quay are the ruins of a house called Gosport; this is a mis-spelling of Goose-port, and a reminder of the days when geese would have been shipped to the west or south of England to end up on wealthy people's tables.

As in previous centuries, Carmarthen welcomed the outsiders who came to the town for a variety of reasons. For example, during the 1940s Belgian troops were accommodated in the town's barracks, and Carmarthen made them welcome by promptly changing all the public conveniences in the town to read Dames and Messieurs. Several of the

THE HORSE FAIR c1950 C31086

One wonders if this 'keep left' sign was adhered to as the farmers jostled for the prize horse and the best price. Next to the monument are public conveniences, now demolished, and below these are the parked buses that had brought the shoppers in to town.

soldiers stayed on and married local girls, and Flemish names can still be found in the telephone directories. Shortly after this, Polish refugees arrived in the town and found work in the farms around Carmarthenshire.

In its issue of 21 June 1940, 'The Carmarthen Journal' reported that 10,000 London children evacuated in the previous September to East Sussex and Kent were to be transferred to the counties of Carmarthen, Brecknock, Pembroke and Radnor. The following week the 'Journal' reported that a large crowd had assembled at the railway station to cheer the arrival of four special trains. One of the more precocious children jumped off the train and asked 'Are we going to have cockles?' while another wanted to know if he could have Welsh rock. One child, on being told that Carmarthen people spoke English fluently, opened his eyes in disbelief, whilst another remarked wistfully, 'I am hoping to learn Welsh.' A year later, the first anniversary of the arrival of the evacuees was celebrated. In the programme (see below), Howard Hayden, Senior LCC inspector for Wales, wrote: 'I remember the day in June a year ago when the unfamiliar green carriages of the Southern Railway steamed into Carmarthen ... Within a week they (the children) were working again in school, and now they are as proud of Carmarthen as the most jealous of her own people: they frequent her mart and market, they enjoy her fairs, learn her traditions, and have a real feeling for the loveliness of her valley.'

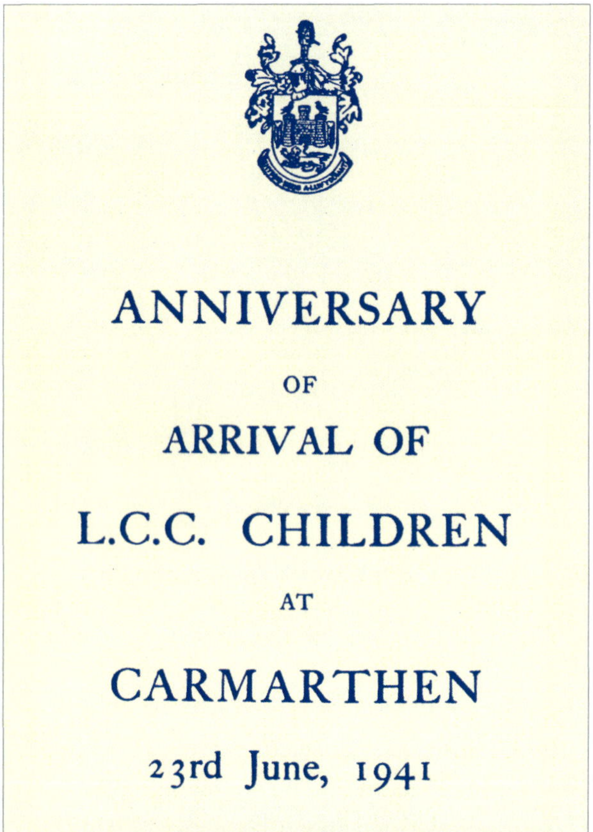
ANNIVERSARY

OF

ARRIVAL OF

L.C.C. CHILDREN

AT

CARMARTHEN

23rd June, 1941

PROGRAMME FOR THE ANNIVERSARY OF THE ARRIVAL OF LCC CHILDREN 23 JUNE 1941 ZZZ00772 (Reproduced by kind permission of Carmarthen Library)

The South Wales and Monmouthshire Training College, now Trinity College (C31008, C31136), saw big changes when in 1957 it admitted women for the first time. This was a far cry from the 1920s, when a male student caught with a girl in the town would be fined 3d! Trinity College has always had a good reputation for speech and drama, and its broadcast hall (C31008) with its multi-level stage was very modern for its day. Other changes took place, like the regular Student's Rag, and during the 1960s and 1970s students campaigned on behalf of the Welsh language movement, raising the profile of Welsh language and culture. Following the 1988 Education Act, which placed Welsh as a statutory subject on the Welsh curriculum, the college has benefited from funding for Welsh courses. The college teachers were also instrumental in the campaigns which led to the opening of Ysgol Bro Myrddin in 1972. Later, in 1989, the Halliwell Centre with its conference rooms and theatre was opened to serve both the college and the community. Trinity College provides a wide range of undergraduate and post-graduate degree courses as well as teacher training, and recently Irish students joined the college population of over 1,700

THE BROADCAST HALL, TRINITY COLLEGE c1950 C31008

TRINITY COLLEGE c1960 C31136

Here we see some of the halls of residence that have been added to the campus.

NOTT SQUARE c1965 C31140

The white building third from the left is the popular Conti's fish and chip restaurant. Angelo and his two brothers came to Carmarthen in the 1920s, and at one time had three businesses in the town, including this fish and chip restaurant. Family members still live in the town today.

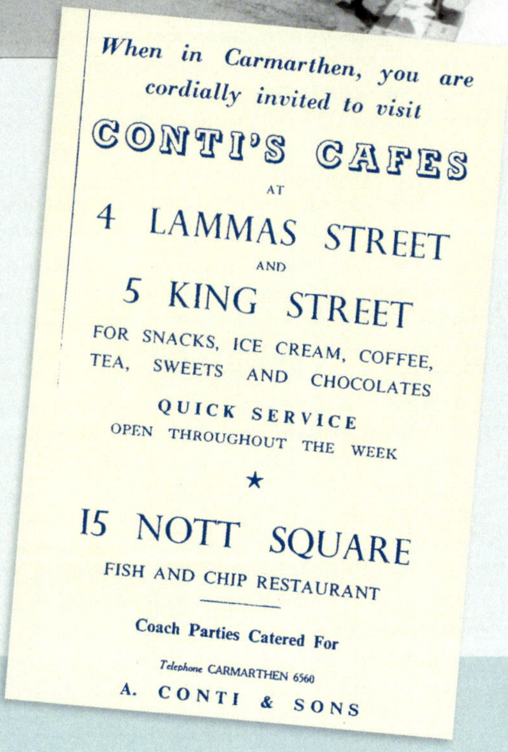

ADVERTISEMENT FOR CONTI'S CAFÉS c1930
ZZZ00773 (Reproduced by kind permission of the Town Council)

The 1950s and 1960s also saw an influx of art students who enrolled at the Art School, then situated in a former mansion called Ucheldir above Picton Avenue (today the Fire Brigade Headquarters is situated there). The local people of Carmarthen were bemused by these ultra-modern art students with their colourful clothes and bouffant hairstyles, and by some of the hippies who on hot summer days went bare-foot about the town. They frequented places like the Plume of Feathers in St Mary's Street and Conti's cafés in Nott Square (C31140), King Street and Lammas Street, and they listened to Elvis's music in Lodwick's Gift Shop in King Street – at that time, King Street offered shoppers plenty of choice (C31060).

CARMARTHEN'S COAT OF ARMS 2004 ZZZ00774
(Reproduced by kind permission of the Town Council)

KING STREET c1955 C31060

KING STREET 1959 C31120

Note the car, so typical of the period, outside Boots – its façade is typical of the period too.

CASTLE HILL c1955 C31096

CARMARTHEN'S COAT OF ARMS ON A MODEL OF A BRITISH BRONZE POT c1900 ZZZ00775

This postcard, sent in c1900, shows the arms without the coracle, a relatively modern addition.

Carmarthen's coat of arms (see page 93) was granted to the borough by the College of Heralds on 9 April 1936, although it was used by the council before this date. The centre of the crest is based on the original seal. The two birds, traditionally regarded as the ravens of Sir Rhys ap Thomas of Dynevor, but now described as choughs, face outwards on the state sword and the Mayor's chain, but face inwards on the maces and the coat of arms.

The present bridge into the town (C31092), which replaced the old stone seven-arched bridge, demolished in 1936, opened on 4 April 1938. At the same time a new road was constructed to Penymorfa, and Castle Hill wall (C31096) was set back a distance of thirty feet.

THE BRIDGE c1950 C31092

Our present Queen first visited Carmarthen as Princess Elizabeth in August 1947 for the first post-war show of the Royal Welsh Agricultural Society. The weather was warm and dry, and the people of Carmarthen gathered from dawn to have a close up view of the 'second lady of the land' whose recent romance had captured the hearts of the people of Wales after the austere years of the war. Everyone was disappointed that owing to his naval duties Phillip Mountbatten could not be with her. The bells of St Peter's rang out to greet the princess; her journey, according to 'The Carmarthen Journal', took her past the 'impossible pile' of the County Council building (C31070, C31043), which was then near completion after the war-time interruption. The building was begun in 1938, but it remained unfinished until the end of the Second World War. The eye-catching chateau-style building was designed by Percy Thomas, who was later knighted for his services to architecture.

In 1951, the Lord Chancellor took the decision that Carmarthen should no longer have a separate Commissioner of the Peace and Quarter Sessions, thus also depriving the town of its Recorder and Clerk of the Peace. The Recorder and Clerk followed the Sword of State for the last time on 17 June 1951 in a ceremonial procession to Penuel Baptist Chapel, where the civic service was held on Mayor's Sunday. This ended a tradition that went back 400 years to the 1546 charter of Henry VIII. With the1972 Local Government Act, Carmarthen lost its borough status and many of its responsibilities to the newly formed District Council. The mayor is now known as the Town Mayor.

THE COUNTY COUNCIL OFFICES 1949 C31070

The old pump house next to Towy Works Ltd is now demolished, and Coracle Way leads down to the quay.

THE COUNTY COUNCIL OFFICES 1949 C31043

In 1958, 'The Girls Gram', as it was affectionately known throughout the town, moved to new premises in Llansteffan Road, which were formally opened by HM Queen Elizabeth the Queen Mother in May 1959. The school was re-named Queen Elizabeth II Grammar School for Girls. In September 1978, the school became a mixed comprehensive and became known as the Queen Elizabeth Cambria School. When the school moved to Johnstown, the Boys' Grammar School took over the building, but unfortunately the oldest part of the school buildings was severely damaged by fire in 1969. To mark the 400th anniversary of the founding of the Boys' Grammar School, a formal visit was made on October 1976 by Her Royal Highness the Duchess of Gloucester, who represented the Queen. A service followed at St Peter's Church, but the celebrations were tinged with sadness: with the introduction of comprehensive education, the school was scheduled to close in September 1978.

A more recent addition to Carmarthen Park are the Gorsedd Stones (C31743k) marking the site of the National Eisteddfod proclamation ceremony in 1973, in preparation for the National Eisteddfod in 1974. Carmarthen had been host to the Eisteddfod on four previous occasions, 1541, 1819, 1867 and 1911.

CARMARTHEN PARK, THE GORSEDD STONES 2004 C31743k (Conrad Hughes)

QUEEN ELIZABETH GRAMMAR SCHOOL HARRIERS 1958 ZZZ00776
(Reproduced by kind permission of Bryan Brinley Richards)

Carmarthen entered the history books again in 1966 when Gwynfor Evans, born in Barry, and brought up in Carmarthenshire, became the first Plaid Cymru member - the Party of Wales - to be elected to Parliament following the death of Lady Megan Lloyd George. A year later the Labour government passed its first Welsh Language Act, which ensured that the use of Welsh was accommodated for in the law courts and public

PROGRAMME FOR THE EISTEDDFOD 1974
ZZZ00777 (Reproduced by kind permission of Carmarthen Library)

administration. Few Welshmen have done more to promote the cause of Welsh nationalism and to preserve Welsh language and culture, ensuring that it has survived into the 21st century. He campaigned to improve road networks between Wales and England, and the main outcome of this was the construction of the M4 motorway through Wales. He lost his seat in 1970, and tried to regain it in February 1974, but he lost by just 3 votes; he regained his seat in the October election, only to lose it again in 1979, and he stepped down as president of Plaid Cymru in 1981. Gwynfor Evans continued to prove a powerful force even outside parliament: in 1980 he pledged to starve to death if the new Thatcher Conservative government did not reverse its decision against setting up a Welsh language television channel. Shortly before the appointed day, Margaret Thatcher backed down and gave the go-ahead for the creation of SC4. The 2001 census showed that the number of Welsh speakers has increased and centuries of decline halted, thanks to the initial efforts of Gwynfor Evans.

The Young Oak

In 1978 it was decided to remove the old oak tree from the junction of Priory Street and Old Oak Lane. For many years it had been nothing more that a withered stump, encased in concrete and surrounded by iron railings. The town, thinking of Merlin's prophecies, held its breath; to be on the safe side, another oak was planted in front of the Roman amphitheatre.

THE YOUNG OAK, PRIORY STREET 2004
C31744k (Conrad Hughes)

Carmarthen successfully prevented a nuclear bunker being built in the town after the Home Office had encouraged the Council with a 75% grant. Work began, but in September 1985 local peace protesters occupied the site and work stopped. A 12ft spiked fence was erected, but the protestors obtained a high court injunction preventing work on the grounds that no planning permission had been sought. In the following December the Council gave themselves the necessary permission, and work began again. During another demonstration in January 1986 peace protesters climbed the security fence, and several were injured, including a woman who lost a finger. With the cessation of the Cold War, government policy changed; the bunker has never been used, remaining an empty underground site to this day.

Carmarthen's sporting traditions have deep roots. 'Come on the Town,' 'come on the Athletic', or 'come on the Quins' are cries often heard from autumn to spring in the town. Carmarthen RFC was founded in 1874, and it is recorded that an away trip in 1877 to Cardigan via Llandyssul by train and then by horse bus took fourteen hours! The club's most famous celebrities are T E Jones, Delme Thomas and Ieuan Evans, who have all become British Lions. Carmarthen Athletic Rugby Football Club is the other rugby club in the town. It currently plays in the Lloyds TSB Division One, fielding two senior sides, a youth XV and under 8s juniors through to the under 16s team. The club was founded in 1944, and the 1st XV reached the final of the west Wales (Tovali) Cup on four occasions, and were the winners in 1985 and 2001, whilst the Youth XV won the Esso Welsh Youth Cup at Cardiff Arms Park in 1993. The club achieved its highest honours in 2002-2003 by being crowned Lloyds TSB Division Two Champions, and during the 2003-2004 session the Second squad (known as the Druids) successfully swept the board by winning Section 'C' of the Llanelli and District Rugby Union, the Champions Cup, the Sprint X Cup and the Lady Howard Cup. They were elevated to the Naylor Drainage League following a play-off victory over their Swansea counterparts, Waunarlwydd, and are looking forward to another successful season. Ten Carmarthen players have progressed to represent Wales at senior level, and three, Delme Thomas (1964, 1968, 1971), Gerald Davies (1966) and Roy Bergiers (1974), have had the distinction of representing the British Lions on tours of Australia, New Zealand and South Africa.

The club appears in the Guinness Book of Records for having the world record collection of sporting memorabilia. In the club's museum there are over 180 international club jerseys (see page 101) and 140 pairs of sporting footwear

THE RUGBY GROUND, CARMARTHEN PARK 2004
C31745k (Conrad Hughes)

This rugby ground within the cycle track at Carmarthen Park is owned by the Town Council, and it is leased to both rugby clubs for their respective first team home games every season.

(ZZZ00778) from world-famous sportsmen and sportswomen such as Pele, Sir Stanley Matthews, Ian Rush, Franz Beckenbauer, Ed Moses, Bjorn Borg, Viv Richards, Colin Jackson, Barry John, Gareth Edwards, J P R Williams, Willie John McBride, Philippe Sella, Jack Nicklaus, Lee Westwood, Colin Meads, Jahangir Khan and John Charles.

Carmarthen Town Football Club was founded in 1948, and moved to its current ground, Richmond Park in Priory Street (C31746k), in 1952. The club was elected into the Welsh League in 1953, and gained promotion from Division Two in 1960. In 1966 Carmarthen won the Welsh League and the Cyril Rogers Cup, and in 1996 won promotion to the League of Wales. The club has established a reputation for the improvement and development of local youngsters, the most notable being Mark Delaney, now of Wales and Aston Villa. In 1999 Carmarthen reached the Welsh Cup Final, but lost on penalties to Inter Cardiff. In the 1999-2000 season the club finished in 4th place in the League of Wales, but this was bettered in 2001 with a third place finish and European qualification. At the end of the 2001-02 season, Alan Latham, the long-serving secretary, retired.

SPORTING SHOE COLLECTION, CARMARTHEN ATHLETIC RFC MUSEUM 2004 ZZZ00778 (Reproduced by kind permission of David Jones, Cyhoeddiadau Cadno)

JERSEY COLLECTION, CARMARTHEN ATHLETIC RFC MUSEUM 2004 ZZZ00779 (Reproduced by kind permission of David Jones, Cyhoeddiadau Cadno)

RICHMOND PARK, PRIORY STREET 2004 C31746k (Conrad Hughes)

But Carmarthen is not only about rugby and football. The Wanderers Cricket Club, based at Trinity fields, play through the summer, whilst those who enjoy a game of bowls are accommodated at the excellent indoor and outdoors facilities in the park. Athletes and cross-country runners enjoy the town's support with international competitions held at the Johnstown running track.

This series of ceramic tile murals was made in 1993 to commemorate the completion of a refurbished shelter at a bus stop near St Peter's Church. They illustrate the history of the town, and were jointly funded by Carmarthen Civic Trust and Carmarthen District Council.

TILE MURAL, CHURCH STREET, 2004 ZZZ00780, ZZZ00781, ZZZ00782 (Conrad Hughes)

In September 2000 some interesting relics were unearthed at St Peter's Church (77296) by archaeologists who were excavating prior to building work. In the chancel they found the grave of Charlotte Augusta Catherine Dalton, who died in 1832 at the age of 27 (C31747k). She was the granddaughter of King George III and his first wife, Hannah Lightfoot, whom he married in 1759. Sharing her tomb is her niece Margaret Augusta Prytherch (who died in 1839 aged 8), great-granddaughter of the king. The large brick vaulted tomb with a domed roof is situated under the centre of the chancel, and a memorial slab on the floor indicates its location.

MEMORIAL SLAB, ST PETER'S CHURCH 2004
C31747k (Conrad Hughes)

ST PETER'S CHURCH 1925 77296

It appears that George Prince of Wales, barely into his teens, noticed Hannah (who was eight years older) when on his way to the theatre. Their marriage in Kew Chapel on 27 May 1759 was witnessed by William Pitt, the then Prime Minister. The couple had three children, Sarah, George (who took the surname Rex and went to South Africa), and an unnamed son. Two years later in 1762, George (now King George) married Charlotte Sophia of Mecklenburg-Strelitz in a bigamous marriage. Sarah, the daughter from the first marriage, married James Dalton from Carmarthen, who was a doctor and an officer for the East India Company. They had two daughters, Charlotte Augusta Catherine, and Caroline, mother of Margaret Augusta, who married Daniel Prytherch, a mayor of Carmarthen. Another document at Kew purports to be Hannah's will, drawn up at Hampstead and dated 7 July 1762, and here Hannah signs the document as Hannah Regina. Again the witness is William Pitt. The will states: 'I recommend my two sons and my daughter to the kind protection of their royal father my husband, His Majesty George the Third, bequeathing whatever property I may dispose of to such dear offspring of our ill-fated marriage'. Hannah is thought to have died in the 1760s.

This discovery may help to unravel another mystery. A pipe organ built by George Pike on the order of King George III and originally destined for the Chapel Royal was erected by private subscription in the south end of the gallery in 1796. One theory is that the king, feeling guilty at discarding Hannah, donated the organ to St Peter's as a memorial.

During the excavations the archaeologists also found a small engraved lead box containing the head of Sir Richard Steele, the famous playwright, founder of the Tatler, and co-founder (with Addison) of the Spectator and the Guardian. Sir Richard was born in Dublin, but his second wife, Mary Scurlock, was a local woman, and he died in Carmarthen in 1729. His

RICHARD STEELE PLAQUE, ST PETER'S CHURCH 2004 C31748k (Conrad Hughes)

RICHARD STEELE PLAQUE, KING STREET 2004
C31749k (Conrad Hughes)

This plaque was put up on the last home of Richard

remains were originally uncovered in the Scurlock vault in 1876 when the titled floor was being laid, and at that time it was recorded that his skull was in good condition, complete with a wig tied at the back with a black bow. Without removing the rest of the remains, officials at the Victorian Church enclosed the skull in the lead box and reburied it in the crypt. A plaque in Steele's memory (C31748k) was put up when his remains were first discovered.

Earlier this year (2004), the quay flooded yet again (ZZZ00788). This is a regular occurrence, and there are many archive photographs showing the town flooded in the past. At the time of writing plans to improve the quay area, which include a marina and quayside shops with a pedestrian bridge to access the railway station, are in still at the planning and discussion stage.

THE RIVER TOWY IN FLOOD 2004 ZZZ00788 (Reproduced by kind permission of David Jones, Cyhoeddiadau Cadno)

THE RIVER TOWY IN FLOOD 2004 ZZZ00789 (Reproduced by kind permission of David Jones, Cyhoeddiadau Cadno)

CHAPTER FIVE

Brighter Horizons

DESPITE THE downturn in industry during the last century, Carmarthen, with a population of around 16,000, is still vibrant, embracing a blend of ancient traditions with the needs of a forward-thinking and enterprising town. You will still find the odd quaint narrow street and back lane full of individual craft shops displaying Celtic jewellery, Welsh woollen goods, wood carvings and local pottery, which is the essence of a bygone era (C31752k). But sitting happily alongside is a modern £15 million redevelopment programme that includes a shopping centre with well-known High Street names. On the edge of the town is a modern leisure centre with excellent all-weather facilities to please everyone, including a 48-station health and fitness club, two tanning units, an athletic track, floodlit pitches, and an indoor soft play area catering for activities such as basketball, tennis, and swimming.

Did you know?

In the 1960s the market attracted many of the new age travellers who had settled in and around Talley, claiming that Carmarthen had a special spiritual atmosphere. They brought an almost eastern bazaar presence to the town with their hippie clothes and home-made crafts, as well as silver and beaded jewellery.

At the heart of the town is its biggest attraction, the famous market (C31753k). It is colourful and full of energy, alive with the chatter of the native tongue, attracting people from the surrounding communities as well as the visitor. In H V Morton's book 'In Search of Wales' (Methuen 1932) he describes Carmarthen as 'the most vivacious market town I had seen in Wales', and having 'the expression of a fat harvest-field on a sunny afternoon'. What a perfect analogy: it sums up the town with its rich history and the relaxed cheery disposition of its inhabitants.

The market is open six days a week, with the main market days on Wednesday and Saturday. In the outdoor market, trestle tables bow under the weight of crockery, carpets and clothes for sale, whilst indoors a vari-

BRIDGE STREET 2004 C31752k (Conrad Hughes)

One of the narrow streets that remind us of a bygone Carmarthen.

ety of Welsh produce such as cheese, butter, bacon, ham, and fresh fruit and vegetables can be found. Around the outside perimeter of the outdoor markets are little shops selling anything from fresh fish to jewellery and clothes to antiques.

OUTDOOR MARKET 2004 C31753k (Conrad Hughes)

This photograph was taken early one Wednesday morning before the crowds arrived.

CARMARTHEN OUTDOOR MARKET 2004 ZZZ00790
(Reproduced by kind permission of David Jones, Cyhoeddiadau Cadno)

Linda and Ray Rees belong to a family of fishermen who have fished on the Towy for generations. They have a shop at Carmarthen outdoor market, and happily serve customers with fish that Ray, a coracle fisherman, has caught locally.

CARMARTHEN INDOOR MARKET 2004
C31755k (Conrad Hughes)

The market site was once called Parc-y-felfed (velvet fields). The market has been here since 1846, when it was decided to put an end to the centuries-old custom of goods being sold in various parts of the town. It opened on Saturday 1 August 1846, and the following year the cattle mart and new slaughter house were built across Catherine Street in Pentrefelin fields. In 2001 the cattle mart moved just outside the town on the St Clears road. The only remaining feature of the original market is the clock tower housing the market offices (C31757k). This was restored when a new larger market was built in 1981.

CARMARTHEN INDOOR MARKET 2004
C31756k (Conrad Hughes)

Fruit, vegetables, butter, and cheese are amongst the locally-grown produce on sale.

THE CLOCK TOWER 2004 C31757k (Conrad Hughes)

ENTRANCE TO THE PROVISION MARKET 2004
C31758k (Conrad Hughes)

This photograph and the previous one were taken at evening after the market had closed.

However, as this book goes to print a cloud hangs over the ancient market, as plans to redevelop both the old livestock market site and the provision market will entail a temporary closure. The clock tower will remain, and a new alleyway of shops will be created from Red Street to Fair Lane, along with a multiplex cinema, a Debenham's store with a bowling alley above, and a multi-storey car park. There is much controversy in 'Merlin's town' about the plans, and discussions are currently taking place which will affect the market traders and their livelihood, and will have implications for a market which has been part of the town for 2,000 years. If the plans are approved, the scheme would be completed by 2008.

Just outside Carmarthen there are many attractions for both visitors and townspeople to enjoy. About a mile east of the town at Abergwili is Carmarthen's museum. It is housed in what was once the palace of the bishops of St David's, and it contains a treasure-trove of artefacts.

Three miles north of Carmarthen at Bronwydd is Gwili Railway one of the few standard gauge preserved steam railways still operating in Wales. It follows part of the original main line between Carmarthen and Aberystwyth that once formed a continuous link between north and south Wales. It was built originally by the Carmarthen and Cardigan railway company and the Manchester and Milford Railway Company, which were eventually taken over by the Great Western Railway. Both passengers and locally-produced goods such as wool, livestock, milk, and timber were carried on this line until the infamous Beeching cuts. Passenger traffic ceased in December 1964, and the last train operated on the line in September 1973.

A Historic Locomotive

Locomotive 'Welsh Guardsman/Gwarchodwr Cymreig' stands at Llwyfan Cerrig station during the December 2003 Santa Specials. This is a Robert Stephenson and Hawthorn Austerity 0-6-0 saddle tank No 715167170 of 1944. It was built for the Ministry of Defence, but it did not join the war effort in Europe. Instead it entered service in the Northumbrian coalfield, later transferring to west Wales. After being withdrawn from service and a spell stored as a source for spares, it arrived at Gwili railway, where it received a three-year refurbishment at a cost of £25,000. It was named in a bi-lingual ceremony in June 1993, though it had hauled a demonstration freight train and worked some Santa Specials the previous year.

THE GWILI RAILWAY 2003 ZZZ00791 (Reproduced by kind permission of G Richards, Publicity Officer, Gwili Railway)

Recently a further half-mile extension was built by volunteer labour to a new station at Danycoed, and there is a more ambitious plan to extend the line southwards towards the former Abergwili junction with a new station adjacent to the Eastern Bypass. Here it is planned to build a cafeteria, a small museum and a carriage-shed – this will almost certainly result in the company employing staff for the first time. Events such as 'A Day Out With Thomas', 'Learn with Thomas', Santa Specials and the summer jazz and rock 'n roll buffet trains account for more than half the annual passenger figures. Families return each year, especially for the Santa Specials, which have run for the last 10 years with seasonal refreshments and presents for the children. The railway has featured in several films, and in Welsh language channel S4C documentaries and period dramas. On New Year's Eve 2004, a dramatised version of the novel 'Carrie's War' (which told the story of wartime evacuees being brought from London to Wales) was shown on BBC television. The railway scenes were filmed on the Gwili Railway, with a former Great Western Railway locomotive imported for the occasion to add realism to the 1940s scenes.

KING STREET 2004 C31761k (Conrad Hughes)

THE GWILI RAILWAY 2003
ZZZ00792 (Reproduced by kind permission of P G Wright, Gwili Railway)

The Council have done a great deal to improve the town. As this book is being written, discussions are going on to obtain European funding to enhance the town gateways. The main gates into the park have been restored and painted, whilst the bandstand has also been painted. Plans to improve the streets from the centre outwards have been laid, and King Street has recently been the first to be re-paved (C31761k).

The town has just seen its second spectacular eight-day Merlin Festival, called the Merlin, Magic and Mystery Festival (ZZZ00783), which was set up to promote Carmarthen internationally. Carmarthenshire County Council teamed up with Carmarthen Cham-

Did you know?

Since Carmarthen is an agricultural town, it is hardly surprising to learn that the Council is supporting a local group of the Slow Food Movement. This group promote healthy eating through traditional recipes, wholesome produce, and food festivals.

COVER OF MERLIN FESTIVAL PROGRAMME 2004
ZZZ00783 (Reproduced by kind permission of the Town Council)

ber of Trade, the Town Council, Town Forum and Carmarthenshire Tourist Association for the extravaganza. Fun commenced on Friday 4 June with a show, 'A Touch of Magic', with Mike Doyle and friends at the Lyric Theatre. Former Wales and British Lion star Ieuan Evans hosted a series of events, whilst an Opportunity Knocks-style event called Magic Moments was staged in Guildhall Square by Carmarthen's own Opportunity Knocks winner Mike Doyle. On the ancient site of the medieval market in Nott Square and at St Peter's Civic Hall a 'cultural village' included arts and pottery, a well-stocked food hall, and for the young Harry Potter fans a parade of look-alikes. To celebrate Carmarthen's past, exhibitions were staged of traditional Welsh dancing, singing and music; there was a carnival queen competition, and there were also living statues, stilt-walkers, magicians, and jesters. Future plans to promote the town include a Winter Festival to coincide with the switching on of the Christmas lights.

The Oriel Art Gallery at the Old School of Art is more than just a gallery; it is actively promoting Welsh artists. It organises an exciting programme of educational events, such as supporting a resident artist at local schools and community groups, as well as presenting talks by artists, and providing workshops in the gallery studio for adults and children. The gallery also organises touring exhibitions, and it has an ever-varied display (it changes approximately every six weeks) of contemporary arts and crafts from new and established artists from across the UK.

DISPLAY AT THE ORIEL GALLERY 2004
C31762k (Conrad Hughes)

THE LESNEVEN SLATE INSIDE ST PETER'S CIVIC CENTRE 2004 ZZZ00784 (Conrad Hughes)

Carmarthen has a rich history and culture to celebrate, and this book is only able to paint a very small portrait of a town that has seen and done so much. It is still building on its foundations, looking forward to a bright future, and no doubt will still add much colour to the history books for many generations to come.

Perhaps we should end our celebration of the town with Merlin the Magician, back at the quay with all its memories of sea-faring days, ship building and excursions to places near and far. In 1995 local man David Jones was challenged to write a song without mentioning the Old Oak. The result was recorded by a local duo called Side FX and launched by the Dyffryn Tywi Male Voice Choir at a concert in the Lyric, some six years ago. It has also been published by Anchor Books.

Twinning with Lesneven & As Pont de Garcia

Carmarthen was twinned with Lesneven in Brittany in 1982, and when the new southern by-pass of the town was completed, the bridge over the River Towy was called Pont Lesneven. Carmarthen is also twinned with As Pont de Garcia Rodriguez in north-west Spain – the Spanish town was already twinned with Lesneven. This twinning took place after the towns discussed the idea in August 2000. Twinning enables towns to make friends, to share ideas and to explore each other's regions, as well as to make contacts for European projects. Carmarthen Twinning Association is very active in promoting the interchange, and arranges for pupils, groups, families and individuals to make exchange visits.

DAWNSWR TIPYN O BOPETH (BITS AND PIECES) DANCING IN LESNEVEN TO CELEBRATE THE 20TH TWINNING ANNIVERSARY 2002
ZZZ00793 (Reproduced by kind permission of Dawnswyr)

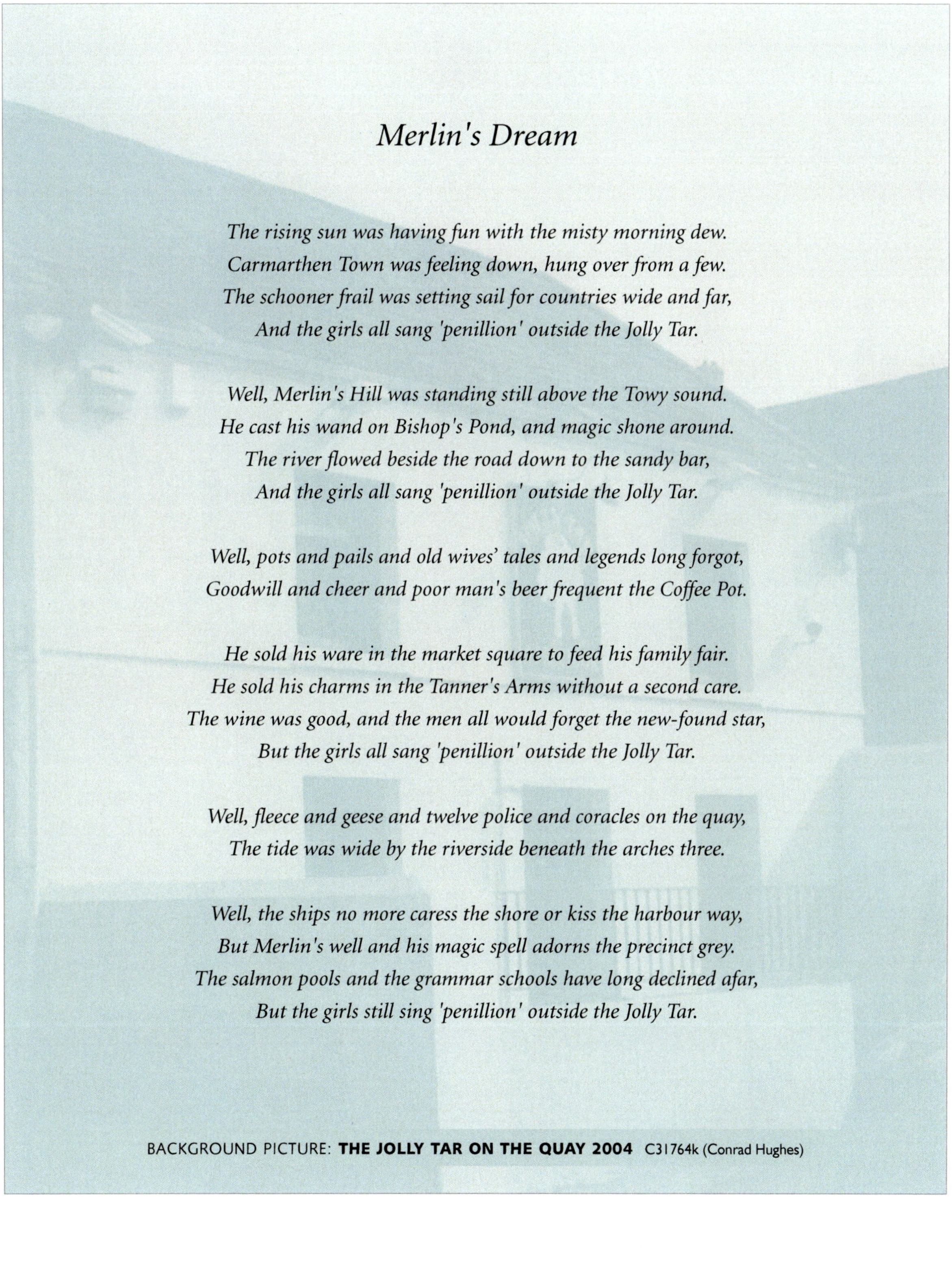

Merlin's Dream

The rising sun was having fun with the misty morning dew.
Carmarthen Town was feeling down, hung over from a few.
The schooner frail was setting sail for countries wide and far,
And the girls all sang 'penillion' outside the Jolly Tar.

Well, Merlin's Hill was standing still above the Towy sound.
He cast his wand on Bishop's Pond, and magic shone around.
The river flowed beside the road down to the sandy bar,
And the girls all sang 'penillion' outside the Jolly Tar.

Well, pots and pails and old wives' tales and legends long forgot,
Goodwill and cheer and poor man's beer frequent the Coffee Pot.

He sold his ware in the market square to feed his family fair.
He sold his charms in the Tanner's Arms without a second care.
The wine was good, and the men all would forget the new-found star,
But the girls all sang 'penillion' outside the Jolly Tar.

Well, fleece and geese and twelve police and coracles on the quay,
The tide was wide by the riverside beneath the arches three.

Well, the ships no more caress the shore or kiss the harbour way,
But Merlin's well and his magic spell adorns the precinct grey.
The salmon pools and the grammar schools have long declined afar,
But the girls still sing 'penillion' outside the Jolly Tar.

BACKGROUND PICTURE: **THE JOLLY TAR ON THE QUAY 2004** C31764k (Conrad Hughes)

LAMMAS STREET 1959 C31116t

ACKNOWLEDGEMENTS

This book could not have been written without a great deal of the help from people who gave their time and share their memories willingly with me. Special thanks must go to the following:
Conrad Hughes, who not only walked every inch of Carmarthen Town with me, but took many of the photographs which have enhanced my text, and read my early drafts of this book.
Jenny Gammon, Reference Librarian, Carmarthen Library who always knew exactly what I was looking for, and where to find it.
David Jones, Cyhoeddiadau Cadno who provided me with a wealth of information, some excellent photographs and contacts and allowed me to use Merlin's Dream.
Selwyn Thomas, Acting Town Clerk for enabling me to see Merlin's Oak, and Margaret Evans for her invaluable information.
John E Davies, Carmarthenshire Archive Service.
Geoff Richards for opening my eyes to the joys of Gwili Railway.
Rowland Thomas, Education and Activity Co-Coordinator, Oriel Art Gallery.
Mrs Edna Dale-Jones for her painstaking research into the story of the coffee pot at the corner of Dark Gate.
Bryan Brinley Richards for his childhood memories of Carmarthen and for reading through my final manuscript.
Also the people of Carmarthen and everyone who shared their memories and helped to make the writing of this book a joy.

BIBLIOGRAPHY

Lloyd, Sir J E, History of Carmarthenshire Vol Cardiff 1935
Lloyd, Sir J E, History of Carmarthenshire Vol 2 Cardiff 1939
Lodwick, Joyce and Victor, The Story of Carmarthen, Carmarthen 1994
Molloy Pat, And They Blessed Rebecca, Gomer Press, 1983
Molloy Pat, A Shilling for Carmarthen Gomer Press, 1980
Molloy Pat, Four Cheers for Carmarthen, Gomer Press, 1981
Dyfed Cultural Services, Carmarthen and the Lower Tywi Valley, Alan Sutton Publishing, 1989
Spurrel William, Carmarthen and its Neighbourhood, Dyfed Cultural Services. 1995
Morton H V. In Search of Wales, Methuen 1932
Delaney Chris, Images of Wales Carmarthen, Tempus Publishing, 2003
Milnes, John A, Francis Frith's Carmarthenshire, Francis Friths, 2000
Numerous copies of the Carmarthen Journal
Several copies of Kelly's Directory

If I have inadvertently left any sources out, please accept my sincere apologies.

Francis Frith

Pioneer Victorian Photographer

Francis Frith, founder of the world-famous photographic archive, was a multi-talented man. A devout Quaker and a highly successful Victorian businessman, he was philosophical by nature and pioneering in outlook. By 1855 he had already established a wholesale grocery business in Liverpool, and sold it for the astonishing sum of £200,000, which is the equivalent today of over £15,000,000. Now in his thirties, and captivated by the new science of photography, Frith set out on a series of pioneering journeys up the Nile and to the Near East.

He was the first photographer to venture beyond the sixth cataract of the Nile. Africa was still the mysterious 'Dark Continent', and Stanley and Livingstone's historic meeting was a decade into the future. The conditions for picture taking confound belief. He laboured for hours in his wicker dark-room in the sweltering heat of the desert, while the volatile chemicals fizzed dangerously in their trays. Back in London he exhibited his photographs and was 'rapturously cheered' by members of the Royal Society. His reputation as a photographer was made overnight.

By the 1870s the railways had threaded their way across the country, and Bank Holidays and half-day Saturdays had been made obligatory by Act of Parliament. All of a sudden the working man and his family were able to enjoy days out, take holidays, and see a little more of the world.

With typical business acumen, Francis Frith foresaw that these new tourists would enjoy having souvenirs to commemorate their days out. For the next thirty years he travelled the country by train and by pony and trap, producing fine photographs of seaside resorts and beauty spots that were keenly bought by millions of Victorians. These prints were painstakingly pasted into family albums and pored over during the dark nights of winter, rekindling precious memories of summer excursions. Frith's studio was soon supplying retail shops all over the country, and by 1890 F Frith & Co had become the greatest specialist photographic publishing company in the world, with over 2,000 sales outlets, and pioneered the picture postcard.

Francis Frith had died in 1898 at his villa in Cannes, his great project still growing. By 1970 the archive he created contained over a third of a million pictures showing 7,000 British towns and villages.

Frith's legacy to us today is of immense significance and value, for the magnificent archive of evocative photographs he created provides a unique record of change in the cities, towns and villages throughout Britain over a century and more. Frith and his fellow studio photographers revisited locations many times down the years to update their views, compiling for us an enthralling and colourful pageant of British life and character.

We are fortunate that Frith was dedicated to recording the minutiae of everyday life. For it is this sheer wealth of visual data, the painstaking chronicle of changes in dress, transport, street layouts, buildings, housing and landscape that captivates us so much today, offering us a powerful link with the past and with the lives of our ancestors.

Computers have now made it possible for Frith's many thousands of images to be accessed almost instantly. The archive offers every one of us an opportunity to examine the places where we and our families have lived and worked down the years. Its images, depicting our shared past, are now bringing pleasure and enlightenment to millions around the world a century and more after his death. For further information visit: www.francisfrith.com

FREE PRINT OF YOUR CHOICE

Mounted Print
Overall size 14 x 11 inches (355 x 280mm)

Choose any Frith photograph in this book.
Simply complete the Voucher opposite and return it with your remittance for £3.50 (to cover postage and handling) and we will print the photograph of your choice in SEPIA (size 11 x 8 inches) and supply it in a cream mount with a burgundy rule line (overall size 14 x 11 inches).
Please note: aerial photographs and photographs with a reference number starting with a "Z" are not Frith photographs and cannot be supplied under this offer. Offer valid for delivery to one UK address only.

***PLUS:* Order additional Mounted Prints at HALF PRICE - £10.00 each** (normally £20.00)
If you would like to order more Frith prints from this book, possibly as gifts for friends and family, you can buy them at half price (with no additional postage and handling costs).

***PLUS:* Have your Mounted Prints framed**
For an extra £19.00 per print you can have your mounted print(s) framed in an elegant polished wood and gilt moulding, overall size 16 x 13 inches (no additional postage and handling required).

> **IMPORTANT!**
>
> **These special prices are only available if you use this form to order. You must use the ORIGINAL VOUCHER on this page (no copies permitted). We can only despatch to one UK address. This offer cannot be combined with any other offer.**

Send completed Voucher form to:
The Francis Frith Collection, Unit 6, Oakley Business Park, Wylye Road, Dinton, Wiltshire SP3 5EU

CHOOSE A PHOTOGRAPH FROM THIS BOOK

Voucher *for FREE and Reduced Price Frith Prints*

Please do not photocopy this voucher. Only the original is valid, so please fill it in, cut it out and return it to us with your order.

Picture ref no	Page no	Qty	Mounted @ £10.00	Framed + £19.00	Total Cost £
		1	Free of charge*	£	£
			£10.00	£	£
			£10.00	£	£
			£10.00	£	£
			£10.00	£	£
			£10.00	£	£
			* Post & handling		[p&p]
			Total Order Cost		£

Please allow 28 days for delivery.
Offer available to one UK address only

Title of this book ....

I enclose a cheque/postal order for £ ....
made payable to 'The Francis Frith Collection'

OR please debit my Mastercard / Visa / Maestro card, details below

Card Number:

Issue No (Maestro only): Valid from (Maestro):

Card Security Number: Expires:

Signature:

Name Mr/Mrs/Ms ....

Address ....

....

....

.... Postcode ....

Daytime Tel No ....

Email ....

Valid to 31/12/14

FRITH PRODUCTS & SERVICES

Francis Frith would doubtless be pleased to know that the pioneering publishing venture he started in 1860 still continues today. Over a hundred and forty years later, The Francis Frith Collection continues in the same innovative tradition and is now one of the foremost publishers of vintage photographs in the world. Some of the current activities include:

INTERIOR DECORATION

Today Frith's photographs can be seen framed and as giant wall murals in thousands of pubs, restaurants, hotels, banks, retail stores and other public buildings throughout the country. In every case they enhance the unique local atmosphere of the places they depict and provide reminders of gentler days in an increasingly busy and frenetic world.

PRODUCT PROMOTIONS

Frith products are used by many major companies to promote the sales of their own products or to reinforce their own history and heritage. Frith promotions have been used by Hovis bread, Courage beers, Scots Porage Oats, Colman's mustard, Cadbury's foods, Mellow Birds coffee, Dunhill pipe tobacco, Guinness, and Bulmer's Cider.

GENEALOGY AND FAMILY HISTORY

As the interest in family history and roots grows world-wide, more and more people are turning to Frith's photographs of Great Britain for images of the towns, villages and streets where their ancestors lived; and, of course, photographs of the churches and chapels where their ancestors were christened, married and buried are an essential part of every genealogy tree and family album.

FRITH PRODUCTS

All Frith photographs are available Framed or just as Mounted Prints and Posters (size 23 x 16 inches). These may be ordered from the address below. Other products available are - Address Books, Calendars, Jigsaws, Canvas Prints, Postcards and local and prestige books.

THE INTERNET

Already ninety thousand Frith photographs can be viewed and purchased on the internet through the Frith websites and a myriad of partner sites.

For more detailed information on Frith products, look at this site:
www.francisfrith.com

See the complete list of Frith Books at: www.francisfrith.com
This web site is regularly updated with the latest list of publications from The Francis Frith Collection. If you wish to buy books relating to another part of the country that your local bookshop does not stock, you may purchase on-line.

For further information, trade, or author enquiries please contact us at the address below:
The Francis Frith Collection, Unit 6, Oakley Business Park, Wylye Road, Dinton, Wiltshire SP3 5EU.
Tel: +44 (0)1722 716 376 Fax: +44 (0)1722 716 881 Email: sales@francisfrith.co.uk

See Frith products on the internet at www.francisfrith.com

FREE PRINT OF YOUR CHOICE

CHOOSE A PHOTOGRAPH FROM THIS BOOK

+ £3.80 POSTAGE

Mounted Print
Overall size 14 x 11 inches (355 x 280mm)

TO RECEIVE YOUR FREE PRINT

Choose any Frith photograph in this book
Simply complete the Voucher opposite and return it with your remittance for £3.50 (to cover postage and handling) and we will print the photograph of your choice in SEPIA (size 11 x 8 inches) and supply it in a cream mount ready to frame (overall size 14 x 11 inches).

Order additional Mounted Prints at HALF PRICE - £12.00 each (normally £24.00)
If you would like to order more Frith prints from this book, possibly as gifts for friends and family, you can buy them at half price (with no additional postage costs).

Have your Mounted Prints framed
For an extra £20.00 per print you can have your mounted print(s) framed in an elegant polished wood and gilt moulding, overall size 16 x 13 inches (no additional postage required).

IMPORTANT!

❶ Please note: aerial photographs and photographs with a reference number starting with a "Z" are not Frith photographs and cannot be supplied under this offer.

❷ Offer valid for delivery to one UK address only.

❸ These special prices are only available if you use this form to order. You must use the ORIGINAL VOUCHER on this page (no copies permitted). We can only despatch to one UK address.

❹ This offer cannot be combined with any other offer.

As a customer your name & address will be stored by Frith but not sold or rented to third parties. Your data will be used for the purpose of this promotion only.

Send completed Voucher form to:
The Francis Frith Collection,
19 Kingsmead Business Park, Gillingham,
Dorset SP8 5FB

Voucher

*for **FREE** and Reduced Price Frith Prints*

Please do not photocopy this voucher. Only the original is valid, so please fill it in, cut it out and return it to us with your order.

Picture ref no	Page no	Qty	Mounted @ £12.00	Framed + £20.00	Total Cost £
		1	Free of charge*	£	£
			£12.00	£	£
			£12.00	£	£
			£12.00	£	£
			£12.00	£	£
			£12.00	£	£
			* Post & handling		£3.80
			Total Order Cost		£

Please allow 28 days for delivery.
Offer available to one UK address only

Title of this book ....

I enclose a cheque/postal order for £ ....

made payable to 'The Francis Frith Collection'

OR please debit my Mastercard / Visa / Maestro card, details below

Card Number:

Issue No (Maestro only): Valid from (Maestro):

Card Security Number: Expires:

Signature:

Name Mr/Mrs/Ms ....

Address ....

....

....

.... Postcode ....

Daytime Tel No ....

Email ....

Valid to 31/12/16

Free Print - see overleaf

Can you help us with information about any of the Frith photographs in this book?

We are gradually compiling an historical record for each of the photographs in the Frith archive. It is always fascinating to find out the names of the people shown in the pictures, as well as insights into the shops, buildings and other features depicted.

If you recognize anyone in the photographs in this book, or if you have information not already included in the author's caption, do let us know. We would love to hear from you, and will try to publish it in future books or articles.

An Invitation from The Francis Frith Collection to Share Your Memories

The 'Share Your Memories' feature of our website allows members of the public to add personal memories relating to the places featured in our photographs, or comment on others already added. Seeing a place from your past can rekindle forgotten or long held memories. Why not visit the website, find photographs of places you know well and add YOUR story for others to read and enjoy? We would love to hear from you!

www.francisfrith.com/memories

Our production team

Frith books are produced by a small dedicated team at offices near Salisbury. Most have worked with the Frith Collection for many years. All have in common one quality: they have a passion for the Frith Collection.

Frith Books and Gifts

We have a wide range of books and gifts available on our website utilising our photographic archive, many of which can be individually personalised.

www.francisfrith.com